BAD JOBS

MY LAST SHIFT AT ALBERT WONG'S PAGODA AND OTHER UGLY TALES OF THE WORKPLACE

edited by Carellin Brooks

ARSENAL PULP PRESS

Vancouver

ARSENAL PULP PRESS
103-1014 Homer Street
Vancouver, BC
Canada · V6B 2W9
www.arsenalpulp.com

*The publisher gratefully acknowledges the support
of the Canada Council of the Arts for its publishing program,
as well as the support of the Book Publishing Industry
Development Program, and the BC Arts Council.*

Design by Dean Allen | cardigan.com
Photographs by Diane Dunn
Author photo by Laura Jane Petelko
Printed and bound in Canada

CANADIAN CATALOGUING IN PUBLICATION DATA

Brooks, Carellin.
Bad jobs

ISBN 1-55152-055-9

1. Employment – Anecdotes. 2. Quality of work life –
Anecdotes. I. Title.

HD6955.B76 1998   331.25   C98-910436-2

CONTENTS

DESK

FEED

HELP

Acknowledgements

First and foremost, I want to thank the many people who submitted stories to this anthology. Even if I didn't use them, your true-life tales were inspiring and horrible. Here's hoping for better jobs.

Thanks also to Chuck Bayliss, who, besides asking all the baristas in Seattle what they had their degree in, was a first-class second opinion. I had more help than was reasonable from Gitana, who papered the city, Rolf Maurer, intelligent explicator of what an editor should and shouldn't do, and Brian Lam, the voice of reason.

Finally, thanks to Jake for all the long rides.

Introduction

I FIRST GOT THE IDEA for this book two summers ago. I had just returned from Oxford University with no job, no prospects and, it must be admitted, no degree (unless you count the M.St they give out as a sort of sop to first-year PhDs). I had retired, after months of zombie-like Walking Dead status, from my position as graveyard-shift systems op at a local chatline. (Our duties consisted of taking horny men's credit-card numbers over the phone. The men often tried to chat up the operators, figuring that if we weren't willing, at least we were free. And we spent hours kicking transvestites and underage girls, of which there were a surprising number, off the free, female side of the line.) The next job I was able to secure involved "market research," which is a euphemistic term for what amounts to calling up complete strangers to bombard them with thinly-disguised advertorials on behalf of our client of the moment. ("So would you consider using Redwood Credit & Thrift for at least some of your banking needs in the future? Yes? Which ones?")

The market research gig paid minimum wage, part-time. I still recall the twisted expression on the face of a fellow worker who went through the training with me: when I asked, she spat out that she had a Master's in community planning. Clearly not a place to share my own dashed aspirations.

At around the same time, I met a woman on the beach one morning. We fell into conversation; she told me that she too had that elusive Master's, and that she was working at Starbucks. "That must be awful for you," I said sympathetically. "I mean, with your education and all."

"Oh, no," she said. "It's a great job. You see, everybody else who works there has a degree, too."

There was my anthology, in a nutshell.

I've had a lot of bad jobs, but not a lot more than anybody else I know. At fourteen, I sold carpet cleaning over the phone – okay, maybe "sold" is a tad over-optimistic – which just may be the archetypal bad job. At fifteen, I had graduated to Paul's Meat Market two storefronts over, where I refused to touch raw meat but was comparatively helpless against the musical tastes of my coworkers. Theirs was a steady diet of "new" country, and to this day, I can still remember all the words to "Lucille."

At sixteen, I was fired from the deli counter of a supermarket after many complaints had been directed against me personally. The supervisor said she was letting me go because she didn't think I viewed my job as a long term-career choice.

People often use an educational scale to connote the bad job, so much so that the taxi-driving PhD has become a bit of a cultural cliché. But bad jobs are an insult to anybody who can think, because, as we all know, the majority of work situations view tendencies towards intelligence as a positive threat.

Horrible work isn't, of course, new. Bad jobs have always been a class issue, and a cultural one: Nike would have us believe – probably correctly – that the Chinese assemblers of athletic shoes feel lucky to be earning their few cents an hour. What's happening now is that people who never thought they'd have to settle for a bad job – the kind of situation Camilla Gibb describes in "That's PhD to You" – are finding that's all they can get. The old education/work connection isn't holding up. The various doommeisters are pumping out the labour-market predictors, reassuring us that there is no such thing as a secure job, that we'll all have to become captains of our fate and freelancers of ourselves. What they don't explain, of course, is how we plan lives with uncertain incomes and the unlimited freedom that comes from being able to choose between bad and worse.

But such gloomy musings don't reflect the authors herein, who are often the first to see the silver lining. That's another thing about bad jobs: no matter how horrible they may be to live through, they're often hilarious in the retelling. That may be because bad jobs are everywhere, in the most unexpected places. Whether in that dream invitation to oversee the opening of the new restaurant (shaky financing means they haven't enough money for knives) or the safe and secure position with a major corporation (which has been cited for so many labour-practices violations it's the top story on the nightly news your first day of work), you never know just where or when the next bad job may hit.

Maybe someday we'll all have fulfilling jobs, ones in which our talents are recognized, our triumphs celebrated, and our skills adequately compensated. In the meantime, there's *Bad Jobs*.

Carellin Brooks
Vancouver · Summer 1998

WA

CH

PETER THOMPSON

Daily Solid Occurence Report

MOJO SECURITY
A DIVISION OF WE'LL SLAP YOU AROUND SILLY SECURITY COMPANY

DAILY SOLID OCCURRENCE REPORT

CLIENT: A man with some fine grounds to secure.
ADDRESS: The old M.A.C.U. building.
EMPLOYEE: Peter Thompson NUMBER (7)

PAGE 1 of 1
DATE:
FROM 0900 TO 1500

1 DOORS OR WINDOWS INSECURE ☐	8 ROUNDS MISSED ☐	15 PROPERTY FOUND ☐
2 THEFT / LOSS ☐	9 VISITORS ☒	16 PROPERTY DAMAGED ☐
3 UNAUTHORIZED ACCESS ☐	10 FIRES ☒	17 LIGHTS (BURNT OUT / BROKEN) ☐
4 ALARM SYSTEM OCCURRENCE ☐	11 FIRE HAZARDS ☐	18 PICK UP ☐
5 INFRACTION OF RULES ☐	12 SAFETY HAZARDS ☐	19 DELIVERY ☐
6 MAINTENANCE REQUIRED ☐	13 WASTE (WATER, POWER, ETC.) ☐	20 MISCELLANEOUS OCCURRENCE ☐
7 PARKING LOT OCCURRENCE ☐	14 RUBBISH ACCUMULATION ☐	21 PHILOSOPHISING ☒

EQUIPMENT RECEIVED CORRECT AS LISTED A keys • flashlight c shotgun

NOTE: PLEASE CHECK OCCURRENCE IN APPROPRIATE BOX AND PRINT DETAILS BELOW.

OCCURRENCE NUMBER	TIME	DETAILS
	0900	I am the man, the security man, I'm standing here on the ground solid.
10	1000	I walked around the grounds, and it was all-right.
	1100	These are some fine grounds, and they are secure.
	1200	Lunch. Solid. These fine secure grounds are solid; I am the security man.
9	1300	The supervisor man in his fine car came around, and told me these solid grounds are all-right.
21	1400	I think about these grounds, and walking around, and them being secure. I am the security man.
	1500	I am writing down this report; and I know these grounds are solid, and I am the man, but my time here is up, so I'll put on some big shoes, and walk on home.

EQUIPMENT ISSUED A keys • flashlight c shotgun

SIGNATURE Peter Thompson

FORM 31632 REVISED

NOT GOOD FOR TRANSPORTATION   PLEASE PRINT CLEARLY

RECYCLED PAPER

OK Parking

I AM A WAGE EARNING SLAVE at OK Parking. Every night except Mondays and Tuesdays, from 12 P.M. to 8 A.M., I park cars and bring them out again. It's not bad, despite the pay. There are generally four or five hours with nothing to do on the graveyard shift but read. *Anna Karenina* took me a week, as did Dante's *Inferno. Ape & Essence* and *Farewell to Arms* took me a night. I am expanding myself in a diminutive job. Not everyone can say that. Not everyone wants to.

"Goddamn, look at the ass on that one." It is morning and manager Mike is making his usual appraisal of the various women walking Broad Street on their way to wherever. They're always working women walking on Broad. By 6 A.M. however, the complexion of occupation has changed dramatically.

"Man, I'd like to stick my tongue up her twat and give it a spin. Goddamn cunt, look at the way that ass of hers sways." Mike almost waxes poetical in his good-ole-boy lusticisms. We stand in front of the nine-storey parking lot, he with one hand in his pocket, the other dragging on a Marlboro Light. His belly sticks out and his weight falls on the back of his heels. "Hello, Mrs. Thomas," he leers innocently, reflexively sucking in his gut, bringing his weight to his toes. Mrs. Thomas smiles frozenly without breaking stride. "Have a nice morning," he chirps as she passes. Then, turning back to me, "Man, how that woman would scream if I could get my sausage roll up her."

I don't feel special hearing Mike's confessional stirrings. He seldom talks to me unless it's as co-conspirator in his carnal cravings. I am glad I don't have to be with him long. I imagine he is worse by lunch time.

Old Joe usually stays in the bullet proof booth where I spend the better part of my nights reading. I am careful to hide my books come 6 A.M. when the two of them arrive. I'm told they don't like people who think working here. Old Joe is cranky and as puritanical as Mike is scatological. Last week, Joe caught a whore sucking off some guy in between two cars on the lot and chased them away. Mike hid so Joe wouldn't see he'd been watching.

"Man, how that woman would scream if I could get my sausage roll up her."

Old Joe takes the deposit to the bank every morning promptly at 7:45. It is only a block and a half away, but we all watch out for him as he goes. Old Joe has been robbed several times in similar circumstances and had an eye shot out to show for it. He had it replaced with a glass one that tends to drift off to the side as he talks to you. The glasses he wears reflect this unnatural specimen even more. It's like being face to face with Jean Paul Sartre, though nobody around here would know who that was.

Eight o'clock comes and I leave. It is not a bad job as jobs go. I always look forward to getting home, but I don't exactly dread coming in the following night; I have *Great Expectations* to finish up, after all.

One night after the late night rush is over, I look up from *Black Spring* to see the sexy brunette come for her El Dorado. She's a regular, and always flirts with me a little. She wears low cut dresses with sequiny frills and a fur coat. I like to think she's a lounge singer and not a hooker. In either case she seems like royalty compared to the nighttime girls who waltz through here and set up shop in cars around the lot. I get the brunette her keys and dash up the elevator to retrieve her car. She always gives me a dollar, sometimes five, although in her case, a smile would be enough. I smile too while holding the door for her. She's wearing some backless thing, and she lets the coat slip a little. Mmmmm. I'm glad Mike isn't here. He could really ruin a moment like this. She waves and drives off. I turn back to the booth.

A black guy is standing between me and my bullet proof solitude. He is quite a bit bigger than me. "Yeah," I ask, "can I help you?"

"Hey man, you see a chick come through here? She's small, pretty, 'bout the same shade as me, drives a blue Mustang?"

"I don't recall a car or girl like that tonight." I reach for my keys, edge past him for the door.

"'Cause that's my car she got," he continues. "She got my keys or my ticket or somethin', can you see if you have a car like that somewhere?"

I turn the lock. "I'd need the ticket to find it." I go in but don't turn my back.

A switch blade meets my gut. "Okay, motherfucker, just back up real slow, and I won't hurt you." I back up and around the small booth to the cash register. "Open it and take the money out," he says, looking around nervously.

I do as he says.

"I won't hurt you, man. After you done here, I'll just take you upstairs and leave you there."

I don't like the way this sounds. I was willing to comply before, but now I'm not so sure. I'm halfway through the drawer when the phone rings. We both jump a little.

"I got to answer that or they'll think something's up."

"Okay, just move real slow."

I pick it up, pause momentarily, then bring the phone down on his head. At the same instant, I bring my knee to his crotch. He looks stunned by my attempt, but hardly the quivering, incapacitated mound of humanity I had hoped to reduce him to. I grab the arm with the knife. His arm is like a charged boa constrictor. It's coiled like a tight rope, the veins pumped up, rigid. I manage to turn him around and push him toward the door. I barely have hold of the knife-wielding arm, which he flails at me, taking little slices here and there. I feel blood on my face where he's nicked me. A brief eternity later I have him at the door. With my arms still locked around him I scream: *"Look, you got most of it, now get the fuck out!"* He opens the door and starts out. No sooner do I release him than I slam the door on his leg. So what if his head and balls are made of iron? This, I can tell, hurts.

"Goddamn motherfucker." He turns back at me. *"I oughta kill you!"*

"Yeah, go for it, asshole." Now that he's on the other side of the glass, my bravery is returning, though this is still far from over. He sticks his knife through the door and goes for my wrists. After adding another slice to my arm, I've no choice but to release him. He hobbles off fast. I lock the door, run to the cash register, and hit the alarm. I stand there bleeding, breathing, staring at the remains.

The cops arrive three minutes later. One runs immediately down the street to check the subway. The other asks for a description. Which makes me wonder what the first cop in the subway is looking for.

We drive downtown, getting out several times to check some bars. Nothing. After an hour of this, they drive me back. They ask if I want to come down to the station and look through some pictures. I tell them I don't think it will help and we leave it at that.

Old Joe, as usual, is the first to work, followed minutes later by Mike. They stand around shaking their heads, looking at my drying wounds and the near-empty cash register. "Well, I saved the ones in any case," I say. Their expressions remain unchanged.

"Fucking niggers," says Mike.

"You were stupid to fight him," says old Joe, staring at me with with his one good eye. "He might have killed you."

"I better call All State," says Mike, lighting a fresh cigarette off the one previous.

After washing off the blood, I hang out in front, retrieving the occasional car. I squat against the wall, my space, checking out the women Mike's missing.

I punch out at 8 A.M. and stroll away. It is tough to keep from limping with all those fives crammed in my shoe.

BRUNO NADALIN

Metropolitan Museum Security Guard

Delivering Flyers with Bashō

I HAD ELEVEN BOXES of panty liners tied to the roof of my Rabbit. Two hundred to each box. They slid off going up a steep stretch of the Upper Levels Highway in North Vancouver. I heard them shift, then slide. Then I saw them in the rear-view mirror: twenty-two hundred panty liners strewn all over the road. Refusing to lose their hard-won momentum, the drivers behind me accelerated right on through, sucking panty liners like leaves in their wake.

That was not a good day.

I delivered flyers for two years, from age thirty-two to thirty-four. Working full-time, I made less than welfare, but since I didn't have to declare the earnings I could collect welfare at the same time. So it worked out to about a thousand a month. I delivered Real Estate Weekly, advertisements, catalogues, plus samplers of Mr. Clean, Irish Spring, chopsticks, and panty liners.

Panty liners were good. They were light, unlike department store catalogues: those weighed like slabs of slate. Usually I carried three, four, maybe five kinds of flyers at once, all wedged into my canvas Netmar sack. I sorted as I walked, working by feel, fingers distinguishing the texture of the Red Spot Grocery flyer from the Radio Shack pamphlet from the Future Shop sale ad. Slot one of each into the Real Estate weekly, fold it, then fling. I favoured the hook shot as opposed to the frisbee toss because the contents were less likely to end up all over the lawn.

I was throwing well the day I met an old school acquaintance. I'd hit my stride. I was relaxed and breathing easily.

"Hey, jerk."

The voice. I knew the voice.

"You know what this is?"

I turned.

"It's a mailbox. You know what a mailbox is for? You familiar with the concept?"

He flapped the lid a few times to demonstrate this remarkable device. It was large and brass-coloured.

"I paid ninety-five bucks for it. And you throw your paper all over the porch. It's gonna rain today. This thing's gonna get soaked. What'm I gonna do with a wet *Real Estate Weekly?*"

Let's call him Del Jones. He still had too many teeth, still had his white sweater tied by its arms around his neck, still had his Slazenger tennis racket in its press and still wore those socks with the little white balls at the back of his heels so they didn't slide down into his $200 tennis shoes. The only differences were that he'd permed his receding hair, his Karmann Ghia was now a BMW, and he'd moved to West Vancouver.

Hand up, covering my face, I stooped for the offending paper.

He recognized me.

"Boo-day?"

He still couldn't pronounce my name properly, either. I started walking.

Del Jones followed. "Boo-day! That you? Ha!" He followed me all the way around the cul de sac. "Hey! You on salary? Hey! You got a company bicycle?" Del Jones danced. He hooted and slapped his thigh. "Boo-day! You always were a loser!"

EVEN WHEN not on the job, meeting old acquaintances was awkward.

"Haven't seen you in years. What're you doing?"

"I'm in information transfer."

"What field?"

"Marketing mostly."

"Any openings?"

"Well, it's not for everyone. Lots of legwork."

Or sometimes I just came out with it. "I deliver flyers."

"Flyers?"

"Flyers."

"You mean you're a paperboy."

"That's right."

I SMOKED POT and carried a Chinese umbrella when I delivered fly-ers. On those rainy midweek mornings I fancied myself following in the tradition of the 17th century Japanese poet and sage Bashō. There I was, a zen man walking the earth, poor but proud, a two-toke glide to my stride, at one with the rain sizzling like cicadas in the bamboo, as attuned to my element as a carp to its pond.

"Hey, fuckhead. Get off my grass."

He hooted and slapped his thigh. "Boo-day! You always were a loser!"

Or there were the cigarette-smoking and coffee-drinking women in housecoats threatening to call the police if I stepped across their snapdragons.

Though usually on those midweek mornings the houses sat stoney and shuttered. Uncurtained windows were rare, so when I passed one how could I not glance in? Scenes return to my mind: a lone woman weeping on a flowered couch; a woman watching *All In The Family* while her husband watched the same show on another TV in the next room; or the stupendously fat woman eating eggs while watching a splendidly spandexed lady lead an exercise program.

I saw a lot of houses and a lot of lawn ornaments: concrete lions, jockeys, pink flamingos, cute donkeys drawing carts, and wooden geese madly whirling their wings in the wind. There were fences of wrought iron, fences of wire mesh, picket fences, slat fences, chainlink fences, and high walls with broken glass embedded along the top. And, of course, there were dogs.

Usually they were behind fences, or chained up, but I became alert to the ominous stirring of those chains. A few times, though, I got caught. One morning a German shepherd backed me up against a hedge. It was cold: the dog snapped and snarled and its breath steamed in the icy air. Each time I tried moving, it lunged. Not that I could've got anywhere lugging two sacks full of flyers slung crosswise over my shoulders. I felt like a peasant hauling buckets of water, a saddled mule, a donkey whose panniers were loaded with slate. And the dog wasn't letting me go. A little kid pedalled past, hockey card fluttering happily in his bicycle spokes, two pounds of bubblegum in his mouth. I remembered an incident from my own childhood, one also involving a German shepherd. The dog had tried to hump me. I was four years old and somehow this enormous stinking beast had corralled me in the back lane and begun to hump my leg. Each time I tried pulling away it growled and humped harder.

Thirty years later, however, the humiliation made me lash out. I caught the dog under the jaw with my foot. I was more surprised than it was. It ran. At which point a burgundy El Dorado rolled up, stopped, the electric window whirred down and an outraged matron tore into me, demanding to know why I'd kicked Joey.

"Joey was trying to bite my leg off!"

"Nonsense. Joey is a people dog."

I showed her the teeth marks in my pants.

"You must have provoked him. I'm calling the police." She began poking numbers on her cell phone. I argued but her window whirred back up and she drove away, trailing a pigtail of exhaust in the hard December air. I lumbered off in the other direction, trying to unload as many catalogues and flyers as I could while I hunted for a place to just dump the entire sack and get out of there.

I was known as a "dumper." Clara, who ran the depot, had my number on this. She'd already nabbed me, having had calls from people who'd found entire bundles of flyers in their hedges, their garbage cans, their recycling boxes.

"Now do a good job, okay. I don't want any more calls."

"Okay."

"And don't dump any in the inlet."

Each morning as I backed my Rabbit into the loading dock, she stood there with her clipboard and route maps. As I'd load up she'd watch the rear end of my car sink under the weight.

"That thing's not gonna last."

"It'll last."

"Is that water in there?"

"Yup." The Rabbit had many mysterious leaks that I'd never been able to plug. All winter, up to three inches of water sloshed about on the floor.

"Well, don't get the product wet, eh. Should drill some holes in the floor. Let it drain out."

"Then it'll start to rust."

She leaned to look down the length of the car. "That's all it is is rust."

"This is my office."

"Get yourself a van. Raise your capacity. Then you could get some people under you and just do drop-offs. Move up in the world."

"I like the fresh air and exercise, Clara."

"Don't want to be a paperboy the rest of your life, do you?"

"Like I said, I like the exercise." And I did. Besides, I rarely felt so relaxed as when delivering flyers.

Late that afternoon some joy-riding teenagers threw a beer bottle at me. It missed and shattered on the pavement. The broken glass under the streetlight made me think of a carp pond glittering in the rain. I stopped to admire it. I like to think Bashō would have done the same.

HAL NIEDZVIECKI

Stupid Jobs Are Good to Relax With

SPRINGSTEEN KICKED OFF his world tour in Toronto's Massey Hall a while back. Along with record company execs and those who could afford the exorbitant prices scalpers wanted for tickets, I was in attendance. As Bruce rambled on about the plight of the itinerant Mexican workers, I lolled in the back, my job, as always, to make myself as unapproachable as possible – no easy feat, trapped as I was in a paisley vest and bow-tie combo. Nonetheless, the concert was of such soporific proportions and the crowd so dulled into pseudo-reverence that I was able to achieve the ultimate in ushering – a drooping catatonia as close as you can get to being asleep while on your feet.

But this ushering nirvana wouldn't last long. For an usher, danger takes many forms: wheel-chair-bound patrons who need help going to the inaccessible bathroom, vomiting teens, and the usher's worst nemesis, the disruptive patron. And yes, there she was: well-dressed, blonde, drunk, and doped up, swaying in her seat and . . . clapping. Clapping. In the middle of another one of Springsteen's interminable solo dirges.

Sweat beaded on my forehead. Her clapping echoed through the hall. The Boss glared from the stage, his finger-picking folkiness no match for the drunken rhythm of this fan. Then, miracle of miracles, the song ended. The woman slumped back into her seat. Bruce muttered something about how he didn't need a rhythm section. Placated by the adoring silence of the well-to-do, he launched into an even quieter song about an ever more desperate migrant worker.

I lurked in the shadows, relaxing my grip on my flashlight (the usher's only weapon). Springsteen crooned. His guitar twanged. It was so quiet you could hear the rats squirreling around the ushers' subterranean change rooms. The woman roused herself from her slumber. She leaned forward in her seat, as if suddenly appreciating the import of her hero's message. I wiped the sweat off my brow, relieved. But slowly, almost imperceptibly, she brought her arms up above her head. I stared, disbelieving. Her hands waving around in the air until . . . boom! Another song ruined, New York record execs and L.A. journalists distracted from their calculations of Bruce's net worth, the faint cry of someone calling: Usher! Do something!

Listen, she slurred. I paid three hundred dollars to see this. I can do what I want.

FOR several years now, I have relied on stupid jobs to pay my way through the world. This isn't because I am a stupid person. On the contrary, stupid jobs are a way to avoid the brain numbing idiocy of full-time employment. They are the next best thing to having no job at all. They will keep you sane, and smart.

I'm lazy sometimes. I don't always feel like working. On the stupid job, you're allowed to be lazy. All you have to do is show up. Hey, that's as much of an imposition on my life as I'm ready to accept. Does The Boss go to work everyday? I don't think so. He's The Boss.

Understanding the stupid job is the key to wading your way through the muck of the working week, and to dealing with such portentous concepts as The Youth Unemployment Crisis and The Transformation of the Work Place. So sit back and let me explain. Or, as I used to say: Hi, how are you this evening? Please follow me and I will show you to your seat.

THE REALITY for the underemployed, over-educated young people of North America is that the stupid job is their future. As the middle-aged population continues to occupy all the "real" jobs, as the universities continue to hike tuition prices (forcing students to work and study part-time), as the government continues to shore up employment numbers with make-work and "retraining," there will be more stupid jobs than ever.

These stupid jobs won't be reserved for the uneducated and poor. In fact, the fertile growth of the stupid job is already reaping a crop of middle-class youngsters whose education and upbringing have, somehow, given away to (supposedly) stalled prospects and uncertain incomes. These are your grandchildren, your children, your sisters, your cousins, your neighbours. Hey, that might very well be a multi-coloured bow-tie wrapped around your neck. . . .

I TOOK a few tentative steps down the aisle. All around me, people hissed in annoyance and extended their claws. Clapping woman was bouncing in her seat. She was smiling. Her face was flushed and joyous. The sound of her hands coming together was deafening. I longed for the floor captain, the front of house manager, the head of security, somebody to come and take this problem away from me. I hit her with a burst of flashlight. Taking advantage of her momentary blindness, I leaned in: Excuse me Miss, I said. You can't do that. What? she said. That clapping, I said. Listen, she slurred. I paid three hundred dollars to see this. I can do what I want.

My flashlight hand wavered. Correctly interpreting my silence for defeat, she resumed her clapping. Springsteen strummed louder. I faded away, the darkness swallowing me up. For a blissful moment, I was invisible.

A LOT of young people think their stupid jobs are only temporary. Most of them are right, in a way. Many will move on from being, as I have been, an usher, a security guard, a delivery boy, a data co-ordinator, a publishing intern.

They will get marginally better jobs, but what they have learned from their stupid jobs will stay with them forever. I hope.

If I'm right, they will learn that the stupid job – and by extension, all jobs – must be approached with willing stupidity. Set your mind free. It isn't necessary, and it can be an impediment. While your body runs the maze and finds the cheese, let your mind go where it will.

Look at it this way: You're trading material wealth and luxury for freedom and creativity. To put it simply: while you may have less money to buy things, you will have a lot more time to think up ways to achieve your goals without buying things. You're making so many dollars an hour, but the on-the-job perks include daydreams, poems scribbled on napkins, novels read in utility closets, and long conversations about the sexual stamina of Barney Rubble.

How much is an idea worth? An image? A moment of tranquility? A bad joke? The key here is to embrace the culture of anti-work. In other words, don't let your brain get all used up memorizing the gallery's obscure seating arrangements or how the boss prefers you to drive the route.

Sometime after the Springsteen debacle, I was on a delivery, dropping off newspapers at various locales. I started arguing with my co-worker, the van driver, about work ethic. I suggested we skip a drop-off or two, claiming that no one would notice and even if they did, we could deny it and no one would care.

He responded by telling me that no matter what job he was doing, if he accepted the work, he was compelled to do it right. I disagreed. Cut corners, I argued. Do less for the same amount of pay. That's what they expect us to do, I said. Why else would they pay us so little? Not that day, but some weeks later, he came to see things my way.

What am I trying to tell you? To be lazy? To set fire to the corporation? Maybe. Our options might be limited, but they are still options. Somewhere in the bowels of Massey Hall it has probably been noted in my permanent record that I have a bad attitude. That was a mistake. I wasn't trying to have a bad attitude. I was trying to have no attitude.

FOR a couple of years I hired on as a security guard at the One of a Kind Craft Show, held twice a year in Toronto's Automotive Building at the CNE. Here the middle classes (whoever they are) flocked to buy baubles that were priced outrageously under the guise of being handmade. The most successful craftspeople were the ones who sold items that all looked exactly the same. The Christmas Tree Ornament Lady packed in the big money. What she made in one hour, I made in two days. Her handcrafted mass-produced ornaments were a kind of torpid corollary to the long hours I spent trolling the aisles watching the employed hordes buy.

The people who worked with me were fascinating. We were all university graduates (or students) with artistic pretensions. We loved to tell jokes on our walkie-talkies. There was a lot of pot smoking. The use of code words over the radio was predominant. Whenever something had to be done, it was difficult to track one of us down. Many of us were outside in the parking lot getting high. We worked fifteen-hour days. The pay was low, but the hours amassed. I didn't have to explain my stupid jobs philosophy to anyone there. They were way ahead of me. They were my professors. Like the ushers at Massey Hall, they were painters and artists and designers and musicians. But many of them had no skill, no craft: this latter group deserves special mention in the stupid jobs pantheon. These are urban creatures, aberrant socialites well-versed in anarchist thought, the best punk bands in Saskatchewan, and what's on cable at 3:30 A.M. They can't imagine working nine to five, have strange ideas, and probably deserve paycheques just for being their loquacious selves.

What I should have told my friend in the delivery van was that when working the stupid job, passivity is the difference between near slavery and partial freedom. It's a mental distinction. Your body is still in the same place for the same amount of time (unless you're unsupervised). But your mind is figuring things out. Figuring out how many days you need to work to afford things like hard-to-get tickets to concerts by famous American icons. Or wondering why it is that at the end of the week, most people are too busy or too tired to do anything other than spend their hard-earned dollars on junk they don't really need. Personally, I'd take low level servitude over a promotion that means I'll be working weekends for the rest of my life. You want me to work weekends? You better give me the rest of the week off.

Meanwhile, it's not like my life is all that great. I might claim to have determined the best way to live, but I remain – like so many other would-be social engineers – caught in the trap of my own contradictions.

Every year at the end of the Craft Show the worst offenders were barred from ever working the Craft Show again. I didn't get banned. I'm still a little embarrassed about that.

MY father's plight is a familiar one.

He started his working life at thirteen in Montreal. He's fifty-five now. His employer of twelve years forced him to take early retirement. The terms are great, and if he didn't own so much stuff (and want more stuff) he could live comfortably without ever working again. But he feels used, meaningless, rejected.

On his last day, I helped him clean out his office. The sight of him stealing staplers, blank disks, and post-it note pads was something I'll never forget. It was a memo he was writing to his own soul (note: they owe me).

But the acquisition of more stuff is not what he needs to put a life of hard work behind him. I wish that he could look back on his years of labour and think fondly of all the hours he decided not to work, the hours he spent reading a good book behind the closed door of his office, or skipping off early to take the piano lessons he never got around to. Instead of stealing office supplies, he should have given his boss the finger as he walked out the door. *Ha ha. I don't care what you think of me. And by the way. I never did.*

DESPITE his decades of labour and my years of being barely employed (and the five degrees we have between us) we've both ended up at the same place. He feels cheated. I don't.

Termination Letter

Cineplex Odeon Cinemas

, Ontario

January 23/

Mr.

, Ontario

Dear ▮▮

Please be advised that effective January 23,
▮▮▮, your services with Cineplex Odeon Cinemas
will no longer be required.

In view of your transgression of January 22
involving putting up a sign in the men's
washroom instructing patrons "not to eat the
big mints" without authorization, coupled with
previous written warnings of July 15th and
November 22, we feel the relationship you have
with the Corporation can no longer continue.

All monies and documents owing to you will be
available on January 25, 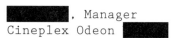.

We wish you every success in your future
endeavours.

Sincerely,

▮▮▮▮, Manager
Cineplex Odeon ▮▮▮

L I

N E

Ice

PEOPLE LOOK AT YOU WEIRD when you're going for coffee wearing winter boots, a touque, layers of sweaters, and carrying a heavy parka . . . in the middle of a summer heatwave. I know this 'cause me and my brother Ash had scored jobs on the afternoon shift at Cataract Ice, an ice factory in downtown Niagara Falls.

There were three main jobs at the plant and we, along with about a dozen or so other petty criminals and generally unemployable characters, rotated between them. At the first and most common job there was a crew of three guys. One would stand at an ancient machine filling bags with ice cubes (not just any ice but *Party Ice!*), while two others would take the full bags from a small conveyor belt and stack them six feet high on wooden palettes. At the filling machine enough ice came shooting out every couple of seconds to fill one bag. Then you had to tear the bag off the rack attached to the machine and slide it through another device that put a metal tie on the top. That metal-tie-putting-on device scared the heck outta me. Gloves or sweater cuffs were forever getting caught up in it and I knew it was just a matter of time before I'd lose a finger or something. If you weren't quick enough tying the bag and then grabbing another one, the machine would spit out another bag's worth of ice onto the floor at your feet. Not only would you eventually get numb feet, but you'd also get the drunken hick foreman, Bob, screaming and belittling you in front of everyone.

I was such a fuck-up that I landed in the block room.

Being in the block room was the equivalent of being in detention in high school. It was a tiny room with just enough space for one person, a skid to stack the blocks on, and the giant block-making machine. Other than that, you were isolated from the rest of the factory. You couldn't hear the blaring classic rock radio station or anything. The only benefit was that in here it wasn't freezing cold, so you could strip down to just one or two sweaters. The block machine was an odd contraption. Regular ice cubes came blasting down this big tube and the machine somehow compacted them into a perfect block of ice, just right for your picnic cooler. That was what it was supposed to do, anyhow. Every so often the machine would fuck up and wouldn't form the ice into a block, at which point the hapless operator had to whack the tube with a rubber mallet, wipe away all the ice cubes that had appeared instead of the perfectly formed block, and then continue making more blocks, bagging and tying them by hand.

I'd throw all manner of stuff into the jaws of that machine: gloves, apple cores, ice picks, whatever tickled my fancy.

My first day in the room was a disaster. I could not get the damn machine to make a block of ice. As much as I'd be smashing the thing with that little hammer, only about every third or fourth attempt produced a useable block. So I just kept brushing away the non-compacted ice cubes and beating the crap out of the machine. By the time Bob stumbled in to check on my progress, I'd bagged about a quarter skid of blocks and I was up past my knees in wasted ice cubes. Bob was pissed. I spent the rest of the day shovelling ice.

On my next shift I had the most fun, albeit most physically demanding, job in the place. The boss gave me a pair of huge tongs, an ice pick, and a weightlifter's belt. It was my job to drag five hundred pound blocks of ice from one room to another. If they weren't perfect I'd have to bust them up with my ice pick and feed them into the meanest, most massive machine in the plant. The main component of the machine was three sets of blades that spun furiously and mashed up anything that got in the way. I'd throw all manner of stuff into the jaws of that machine: gloves, apple cores, ice picks, whatever tickled my fancy. Of course, I wasn't the only one who added special surprises to the production process. One of the old truck drivers was forever pissing in the ice, and we all tossed our smoke butts in there. One of the most rewarding parts of the day came during clean-up. The pieces of ice that were too small for proper cubes were automatically sifted into a huge metal container, the crush bin, over the course of the day. At the end of each shift someone had to hop in the bin with a dirty old shovel and push all the crush out a little trap door so other guys could bag it, to be sold as "Crushed Party Ice!" While in the crush bin you could be seen by no one, so it was fair game. Besides stomping around in filthy boots and a shovel, we all put whatever nasty stuff in there we pleased. Bodily fluids were always welcome in the crush bin. Phlegm was the most common. You'd feel some mild satisfaction knowing that although you were spending your summer in a bleak, grey, frozen hell with a drunken fool bossing you around, some idiot yuppie was sitting on a beach somewhere wondering why his margarita had that slimy feel to it. Ha ha.

One day Bob was just hammered – I'm talking falling-down drunk. He was being a bigger asshole than usual and he fired two guys. Now the place was short-staffed and right after lunch something went goofy with the refrigeration unit. It got above freezing and the whole place started to melt. If we didn't all pitch in extra hard the company would lose thousands upon thousands of dollars in profits that day. Me and Ash split during our coffee break and never went back. Fuck you, Bob.

Me and Mars

FOR SEVERAL months I had a job making boxes – stapling cardboard
into square shapes, stacking them into piles. I sat on a metal stool
in front of the stapling machine, a medieval thing, old and strange;
it looked like an iron stork. By kicking a pedal at its base,
it shot a staple into the cardboard which I folded and turned
quickly like origami in its beak. A light bulb hung on a long
black wire overhead and by the end of eight hours,
the space around me would be surrounded by four walls
of boxes. Near the end of the night and the beginning of morning,
the nightwatchman made the rounds. Before he appeared,
I could hear all those keys on his belt and the flashlight
he carried would creep shadows ahead of him.
His name was Mars. I have run into a Martian wall
in trying to remember him; my memory of Mars is so quiet,
so far away, barely there, held together with strings.
Everything about Mars seems to be covered with sand rust.
I do remember he was Ronald Reagan's number one fan.
He would talk about war and the car he drove (something loose
dragged underneath it and made dangerous red sparks on the ground).

The Hands of Mr. Souza

THE HOUSE IS DARK and still full of sleepers before dawn. In the bathroom the sudden glare of twin fluorescent tubes hits my half-lidded eyeballs like a tossed handful of powdered glass.

My hands are useless lobster claws, all stiffened tendon and tetanized muscle. So like a scrubbed-up surgeon I turn the tap between my elbows, then wait for the steaming water to wash the rigour from my corpsed fingers. Slowly they begin to flex once more – ten little Frankenstein's monsters arising eerily out of stone-stiff sleep. In the mirror I see myself becoming Mr. Souza, becoming an appendage of the crumbing machine he has trained me to control.

For the day's crumbing work, there's no need to unravel these knotted fingers. Two steel flippers at the ends of my arms would suffice, or a pair of hooks, or a tin-woodsman metal gauntlet locked up with rust. But I need my fingers simply to eat a stealthy breakfast in the darkened kitchen, and to drive to the plant through the blissful August air, still unburdened with another morning's stale rush-hour exhaust.

The hands of Mr. Souza, the full-time crumber, have been claws full-time for fifteen years of punching in and out. The Hamilton Street Railway delivers Souza to work; he simply fumbles for a bus pass and doesn't need fingers to drive. When he eats, his two claws come together like two sculpted bronze hands meeting in prayer, one on each side of a capicollo-and-lettuce sandwich from Rosa's Italian Bakery around the corner. The tan crust of the sandwich roll is lighter than the dark weathered-metal colour of Souza's blunt, inexpressive fingers.

Nothing like that hand-kneaded Italian roll – I can see it being made, I retreat to Rosa's myself for lunches when I can – would ever emerge from the huge, aging bread factory where Souza initiates me into the crumbing operation. "Too much fresh, no good. Too much dry, no good," Souza shouts above the din, gesturing at the most recently-rejected stacks of white Wonder bread. Out of the thousands of soft uniform loaves that depart each day in local delivery vans and long transport trailers, hundreds remain behind – outdated, misshapen, sliced lengthwise by mistake. The trays of rejects arrive in tall stacks at Mr. Souza's corner, to wait and grow crusty.

"Too much fresh, no good. But too much dry, burn up inside. See this window? See this line? Keep crumbs inside up to line. Too low, no good. Too high, no good. Too much fresh, no good. Start her up." Souza's head nods three times, and with newly-supple morning hands I punch, in sequence, three large red buttons. A rising whine becomes a roar as the yellow box of the crumber, huge as a house, shakes into motion atop its rubber mounts. Already Souza is plunging his Captain Hook hands into the trays full of half-dried-out loaves, firing them into the gaping hopper that opens into the machine's entrails. The crumber eats loaves at one end, the end where I remain to feed the machine. At the other end, fifteen paces away, sandy avalanches of evenly toasted breadcrumbs cascade into long cast-iron wheeled troughs.

Shouting "keep up with machine," Souza moves to the trough, collects a handful of crumbs, lets it fall between his stiff, brown-skinned fingers. "You make too wet, put too much fresh, she going moldy very fast. Too dry, maybe machine catch on fire, you shut her down with this button. You smell, like burning toast? You press this button. Never go away while machine turn on. Very important. You wait for guy to come give you break. Never turn off when still crumbs inside, only for emergency. You start her up, watch all the time, do good job. Make good stuffing for turkeys – eh? Watch me. Not too much fresh, not too dry, you see like this. You keep up with machine. Keep up with machine."

Mr. Souza flies to Portugal for his holidays. Alone in the corner of the bread factory, away from the winding conveyors of cooling loaves that sift crumbs down through the plant's slanting light, away from the cottage-sized ovens where bakers work with paper towels swaddled around their dripping foreheads and desperately gulp Cokes in a single swallow under floor fans useless against the ovens' heat, away from the bandsaw slicers and pneumatic thrusting bread-bagging robots, out of sight and sometimes unrelieved for hours on end, I feed the crumber one loaf at a time.

Here my hands become claws. Knuckles together, palms out, I puncture the plastic bread wrapper with karate-rigid fingers.

Here my hands become claws. Knuckles together, palms out, I puncture the plastic bread wrapper with karate-rigid fingers, expel the slices with the heels of both hands, toss the deflated wrapper aside. Many times each minute my hands perform the motion by themselves while my thoughts wander, circle, lose themselves. Keep up with machine. Watch line in window. Keep a steady machine rhythm. This is what a machine thinks. Not too high, not too low. In my demonic forge I transmute more than just the stale, rejected, malformed Wonder bread. My body grows machine-like in eight different ways. My own mind and body are stripped, pulverized, left puzzling in a dark corner at the wrong end of a breadcrumb trail.

On the prosperous shady maple and chlorine-blue swimming pool side of Hamilton Harbour, crumbing was a bad job. But here on the blackened-brick, trolley-wired, east-end side of the bay, crumbing was good work. Here you may not have eaten Wonder bread but you really wanted to work in the plant that made it. Here it was a damn good job, but not at first for me, from the white-bread side of the bay and not yet toughened up, though this was something Souza promised. "Machine toughen you up soon, no problem." He was right. By the time Souza returned from the Old World I had grown hardened to my new work.

The Warehouse

"I NEVER, NEVER, RAPED a woman who didn't love it," says François as he comes up from behind and wraps his hairy arms around me.

I say, "Ha, ha, François," elbow him away, and get back to my job.

Every day is different at my job. Some days I use big machines to cut bolts of fabric into tiny squares. Some days I paste these squares onto pieces of paper to make fabric cards. And, more and more since Tony quit and they're short in the back, I unload bolts of fabric off the trucks and stack them.

François thinks it's fun to drive the fork lift toward me at full speed and pin me to the wall, a steel blade on each side of my body. "Take a fuckin' joke," he snarls, his black eyes throwing sparks like the fork lift when he drags it over concrete. Some days François wants to marry me and tries to follow me home. Other days he wants to kill me.

I tell myself I'm an anthropologist. I tell myself I don't belong here. This is not my beautiful life. I'm not like Lola, born and raised in Jamaica, who's been working here for thirty-five years. Not like Rilla, from Poland, who hates everyone who was born anywhere else. Not like Thomas, who, as my boss always tells me, could have done something better with his life – he's a man, a white man, and an Anglophone, for Christ's sake – but didn't. "A waste," says my boss. "What a waste." Not like Ricardo or Manuel, who work illegally and are grateful for their small, regular paycheques.

Most of all I'm not like the people upstairs. Weeks pass without one of us going upstairs, without someone from up there coming down. We don't go up unless they call us. And when they do, it's not good news, and we get chills from the air conditioning and from what awaits us there.

Upstairs the men are the bosses and the girls are the secretaries. The girls are stupid, too, like living stereotypes of secretaries. Or, if they aren't, they persuade everyone that they are, including themselves and me. Which is worse.

> *Upstairs the men are the bosses and the girls are the secretaries.*

MY girlfriend searches the papers every morning, makes calls all day. Nothing. I get up every morning at six, take the Metro to the end of the line, take a bus for twenty minutes more. By June, we no longer go out much. Our evenings are reserved for weeping, she because she doesn't have a job, me because I do.

FRIDAYS are the best. On Fridays, the bosses bring in cases of beer for the downstairs workers. We finish the week in an alcoholic haze, which is good, because the last thing we have to do Friday evenings is coat the floor with a noxious green chemical that reduces dust on the fabric. Lola calls it feeding the chickens. If you don't wear gloves, the powder blisters your skin. But nobody upstairs thinks of providing us with masks, and nobody downstairs thinks of complaining. We drink beer and gather up our things to go home, the chemicals burning our eyes and throats, making us tear up as we wave goodbye to each other.

MY first week Mr. BOSS tried to instill a positive attitude in me. "We have people from fifty different nations down here," he told me proudly. "No affirmative action needed. It's a melting pot, right here. No politics involved."

AFTER looking every day for two months, my girlfriend gets a job. Her job is making sandwiches at a French construction company in downtown Montreal. The shift is from 5 A.M. to 9 A.M. and pays minimum wage, no tips. I feign enthusiasm — now we *both* have shit jobs. It matters to her in a way I don't understand, going to work every day. Whatever. I'm a good girlfriend. I take her out drinking to celebrate. Only we have to be in bed by eight-thirty, so we cut the night short and try to sleep. By four the next morning we are up, gritty and despairing. I walk her to work in the dark, and kiss her goodbye as the horizon is growing light.

"THERE is a black girl moved in my apartment," says Rilla. "I called the management to complain. Nice face she has but such an ugly bitch inside. She hangs her laundry. . . ."

I tune her out, focussing on my little squares of cotton and my pot of glue. Lola comes back in the room with her coffee and Rilla starts humming some cheesy love song.

AT the end of the second week the safety equipment on the cutting machine fails. I whip my hand away seconds before the blade falls. The crash of the broken blade reverberates through the warehouse. The fabric and the board clatter to the floor in two halves. Lola lets out a low whistle. "You okay, girl?" she asks me. Thomas comes over and shuts off the machine, and Rilla pulls out a chair for me. "Sit," she says. "Just sit." I do.

The boss comes down. "That's no good," he says. "We need those samples today. But we can't have you getting your fingers cut off either."

"Thanks," I say. He moves me to the stock room for the rest of the week, just me and François. "Thanks," I say.

I come home that day to find my girlfriend curled in bed, hiding under the covers. I lift them and say hello. She looks at me reproachfully, eyes red-rimmed.

"Something terrible's happened," she says to me. "I lost my job."

I GO to work. My girl is at home, nursing her post-job hangover. She didn't speak enough French, so they fired her. "So what?" I say, and she turns to me in rage: "You don't understand. I have to work."

"Why don't you stay home and write?" I ask. "Take the summer off."

"I can't. I need a job."

ONE of the bosses comes downstairs to pick up an order, and Lola grabs his fat pasty hand and shoves it down the back of her dress so he can feel her sopping back. "Really, Lola," he says, holding his hand limply out from his body, as if contaminated.

"I want a fan that works!" she insists. The boss turns and blows in her face, but she doesn't even crack a smile. Sweat drips from her elbows. He beats a quick retreat upstairs.

"Even my crotch be wet!" Lola calls out to one of the upstairs sec-retaries as we all leave for the night. The secretary covers her red mouth with her red nails and gasps.

WHEN I come home my girlfriend rubs my neck. We give each other pep talks. We go over our budget again and again. We walk together at twilight, enjoying the fragile pastel end of another day. But always, hanging over me like a storm cloud, is the knowledge of the next morning approaching, the fact of the job I have to go to.

I tell myself that I'm doing time, time in the working class, that I'm getting off easy, that I should be grateful for the experience. I tell myself I love my girlfriend and she loves me, that it's all okay, every-thing's okay, as long as one of us has a job.

Hairnets and Giblets

SURE, YOU PULLED A paycheque from it, but how many turkeys had to die first? Three million that summer alone. You had connections in the turkey world. Your father. "That's how you got in there," your mother said, as if wearing a blood-drenched apron every day all day was some kind of privilege. Out, damned-fowl spot and all that.

The hairnet didn't become you, either, or the rubber boots throbbing through grease. But that didn't stop the killing- room guy, the one with the electric knife, from asking you out. What he must have seen: the giblet girl, sixteen and ashamed. So many naked organs everywhere, hearts lying all over the cement floor. Sometimes they threw them, like a food fight. You'd feel the splat of cold heart against your cheek, sliding towards your neck. You couldn't throw them yourself, not because you didn't care for games; you couldn't see whipping hearts at people, even turkey hearts.

At first, you didn't even know what giblets were. You thought they were something rich people drank, not vital organs, livers and such. The killing-guy must have wondered what you looked like under your hairnet. He wanted to take you somewhere beyond the gigantic turkey sign over the factory door on his big bike. He gave your father a note to give you, asking. The note had bits of feather stuck to it, and bad spelling, which offended you, and you in your prim hairnet and your shame told your father to "tell Mr. Ellis no. Thank you." You imagined your father in his rubber boots size twelve bearing the message into the hot killing room, his answer, "Tell Mr. Ellis no. Thank you." You imagined disappointed men. There were three million turkeys that summer. The plant was operating full-tilt, the manager said.

Such a relief to pull off your hairnet, go back to grade eleven. School was such a bloodless place, without rubber boots. But Christmas dinners were never the same for you, after that summer. You'd swallow hard when the glowing, stuffed turkey appeared, laced in parsley and prunes. You swore the words "tell Mr. Ellis no" came steaming forth from the body cavity, everyone famished.

Beet Line

I THREW UP THE DAY they called me to work at the Agripac cannery. I don't remember exactly why. Maybe it was something I ate. Then again, maybe I knew what Agripac was going to be like. All I clearly remember is walking into the lunchroom for the first time with the taste of vomit lingering in my mouth.

It was shift change, and the place was jammed with grim-faced folks smoking cigarettes and drinking cans of soda and paper cups of vending-machine coffee. I didn't know a soul in the room, but they all looked vaguely familiar, like the straight-laced, narrow-minded, hard-working, small-town folks I grew up with – and ran away from, as soon as I was old enough to leave. They scared me to death. I stood among them, reeking of bohemian dyke squalor, wondering what I'd gotten myself into.

It was simple, really. The unemployment benefits from my last shitty job had expired, and I was broke. I'd worked in canneries, off and on, since high school. They hire practically anybody who can walk and breathe at the same time. They don't ask for a resumé, and it doesn't matter what you look like. You just go down and sign up, and if you wait around long enough, and don't starve to death in the mean-time, eventually you get called in to work.

I reported to the office, where they strapped me into a plastic apron that reached from my chin to my toes, handed me a hairnet (which I surreptitiously slipped into my pocket), and sent me to Marge, who was in charge of the beet belts. Marge led me up a short set of stairs to the slice line. We stood shoulder to shoulder without speaking, staring at the worn yellow conveyer belt. There was a tremendous blast from an air horn, somebody threw a switch, and the belt jerked forward. Up the line, washers shook out a steady stream of beets, covering the belt with a thin layer of gleaming purple slices. When the beets reached us, Marge began to pick at them with deft fingers.

"Okay," she shouted, straining to be heard over the machinery, "the bad'ns, them you can't eat 'cause they's rotten" – she held up a soft, blackish slice – "they go down there in your bucket on the floor" – she flicked it away disdainfully – "and the good'ns, the ones you could eat, but they ain't perfect, like they ain't round, or they got some discolour" – she held up an apparently imperfect slice – "they go in that tray on your left" – pointing at a shallow tin tray bolted to the side of the belt, she dropped the slice in. "Them're the fancy."

"The fancy? Then what's left on the belt?"

"*Extra* fancy. Now, you try it."

I picked up a slice gingerly, and dropped it in the tray.

"Now, what's wrong with that'n?" she demanded, retrieving the slice.

"It's not round?" I ventured, tentatively.

"None of 'em's perfectly round! That'n's round enough. Try it again."

This time I snagged an obviously rotten slice, which I dropped into the bucket on the floor.

"Um-hmm, that's right. Now, try to go a little faster." She watched me pick and discard slices for a couple of minutes, then, patting me on the shoulder reassuringly, said, "I'm sure you'll pick it up." and walked away.

I have always hated beets. Passionately. And while I can tell a rotten beet when I see one, I have a hell of a time distinguishing a mediocre beet from a truly outstanding beet – an extra fancy beet. How round is round enough? How discoloured is too discoloured? Damned if I know. In the first ten minutes of that first shift, I made my first professional beet-grading decision. I would concentrate on the rot, seek out the most putrid and pungent, thus avoiding potentially tricky aesthetic questions, without abrogating my responsibility to the public's stomach.

Even with such limited professional goals, this was not easy. Within the first hour, my arms grew heavy, as though I had bags of water strapped to my wrists. Well before the first break, my fingertips began to bleed. I'd scraped the skin off, trying to pluck slick slices from the rough belt, and watery trails of my blood now snaked among the beets. I was immersed in cacaphony – machinery rumbling, water roaring, metal screaming, cans slamming, voices shouting. The raw, rooty stench of steaming vegetable pulp hung in my throat like a fist. I nearly gagged on it. When the first break came, an hour and forty-five minutes in, I staggered on stiff legs downstairs to the lunchroom, slumped on a bench in the corner, and stared balefully at the coffee machine. No one spoke to me, and I spoke to no one. When the air horn signalled the end of the break, I trudged back to my place, the belt jerked forward, and the beets rolled once more.

All that first day, I watched the clock. I didn't know that time practically stops when you pay attention to it. Later, I'd play games with myself, trying to see how long I could go without looking, but that first day, I watched it constantly, incredulous at the impossible length of a single second.

That night, I lay in bed cradling stained and swollen fingers. Each time I closed my eyes, I saw a river of beets. All night long, I graded beets in my sleep, and when I woke the next morning, my hands were curled into arthritic fists.

THE SECOND DAY was much like the first. Every couple of hours, Marge came over and stood next to me, casting a critical eye as I fumbled with the beets. I could tell I wasn't doing very well. I just wasn't fast. I'd start out diligently, but soon my mind would drift. I'd start thinking about something besides beets – politics or girls or poetry or rock & roll or what I was gonna buy with my first cheque – and my hands would slow down and practically stop.

On the third day, I smoked a joint before I went in. It helped for the first hour, when I was mesmerized by the purple beets on the yellow belt, but by the third hour, I was dragging worse than usual. On the fourth day, I did it again and discovered, to my delight, that I could sing along with the machines, harmonize with their high-pitched, minor-keyed whine, and no one could hear me. Clearly, I was cracking.

On the fifth day, I decided to talk. At lunch, I took a seat across the table from a sharp-featured young woman who was holding an enormous sandwich – thick slices of bologna and bright, ruffled leaves of butter lettuce dripping fat drops of rich mayonnaise, enfolded in pillowy slices of Wonder bread. I tried not to stare, but Christ was I hungry! My own lunch consisted of a handful of saltines, a fuzzy chunk of Monterey Jack, an undersized green pepper, and a trio of ancient, whole wheat figbars. Glumly, I fished it out of my tattered brown bag. When I looked up, she was watching with a blank expression.

"Hi," I said.

"Hi."

"My name's Red."

"Oh," she said, "your hair's not red."

"It's short for my last name. Reddick." She thought about that for a minute, then put down her sandwich, reached into her lunch bag, took out a pamphlet, and handed it across the table to me. Flames leapt across the bold black letters: 'Heaven or Hell – YOU Decide!'

"HaveyouacceptedJesusChristasyourlordandpersonalsaviour?" It came out in one long word, like "supercalifragilisticexpialidocious." I set the pamphlet down, stuffed my pitiful lunch back in the bag, said, "Uh, excuse me," stood up, and got the hell out of there. So much for talk.

ON THE first day of my second week, determined to make a go of it, I dressed in clean clothes and left all my drugs at home. Feeling honest and clean and sober, a real working class hero, I strode through the lunchroom, past the supervisors' table, and headed for the lavatory. She came in while I was in the stall. I heard her shoes squeak. When I came out, she was standing by the sink – five feet tall with the body language of an oak, dressed in a starched uniform, her unblemished hardhat perched on a nest of steely curls. It was Lillian. Boss of bosses. The head Floor Lady. Her small gray eyes travelled over me. Then, she spoke.

"Don't you have a bra?"

"Uh, no."

"Well. You'd better get one. It isn't very becoming." She executed a perfect military about-face and strode from the room. I went back in the stall, sat down, and waited for the air horn. After that I wore layers of shirts and stopped tucking them into my jeans. Maybe nobody noticed. Maybe nobody gave a flying fuck. Lillian never spoke to me again, and I never again went to work sober.

Of course, weed is one thing. Speed – amphetamine – is an entirely different matter, and it was speed which hastened my exit from Agripac. A friend gave me a fistful of whitecross tablets. It wasn't that I didn't know better. I did. I just didn't care. I dropped four of them on a Thursday, and by the time I landed at work, I was buzzing like a busted neon sign.

Finally, I was fast. My fingers fluttered like butterflies over the beets, moving with effortless assurance and grace. I giggled, I sang, I laughed out loud, I made speeches no one heard. I outworked everyone else that day. Naturally, Marge noticed.

She came over and stood next to me. I felt proud, like a protégé. She tapped me on the shoulder and when I turned to look at her, she smiled, crooked an index finger, and said, "Come with me. I have another job for you." We went to the end of the line, where six different belts dumped whole beets into thirty-gallon aluminum tubs. She had me fetch a hand truck.

"Now when these tubs get full, I want you to stack 'em three high on that hand truck. You see the fillers over there? I want you to take 'em over there, okay?" I nodded eagerly, thinking, oh boy! A job where I get to move around!

Even in my chemically reinforced condition, I struggled to lift the first tub, then the second. I barely boosted the third to the top of the stack, and when I pulled the hand truck back, the stack swayed forward and toppled over. Beets rolled everywhere. Marge was at my side instantly.

"Now why'n hell'd you do that?" she demanded. I was crawling around on the floor, scooping up beets. "Stop that! Leave it for the clean-up! You got full tubs at the ends of them other lines!"

Sweating and struggling, I managed three more trips before my next accident.

"Well, maybe you ain't strong enough for this job." That made me feel worse than when Lillian told me to get a bra. "We'll have to find you somethin' else to do after lunch."

So, I became a can stacker, taking empty thirty-three ounce cans out of cardboard boxes, stacking them twelve high in alternating rows of five and six, and wheeling them across the warehouse. I did my best, but the speed was burning off, and I developed an ugly case of jitters, resulting in a deluge of dropped and dented cans. This hardly met with Marge's approval, and she put me back on the line for the last hour of the shift. This time, I was in carrots.

Taking speed is like handing your nervous system over to a loan shark. You pay a lot of interest on a bad decision. I crashed hard the next day. My teeth ached, my skin hurt, my eyes wouldn't focus. Somehow, I made it to work, but my fate was sealed when Marge saw me sagged against the belt, nodding off into a pile of steaming carrots. At lunch, she sent me to the office where, to my great relief, I was summarily laid off and sent home.

I have not touched a beet – fresh or canned, whole or sliced – since.

HC

LE

JO ANNE C. HEEN

Shootout at the Triple X

LOVE LOTIONS LINGERIE XXX VIDEOS BACK TO SCHOOL SALE read the twenty-foot-high billboard in the parking lot of the sex shop where I worked the evening shift as a cashier. Broken glass and shell casings crunched underfoot. The oleander bushes at the front of the store were squashed flat, like something big had rolled in them. Garbage was strewn everywhere. An employee of the paint store across the street shouted what sounded like "fucking assholes," but I probably heard wrong. Our front door was wide open, a city violation. As I started to kick it closed, Rob, the assistant manager, stopped me.

"Leave it open," he called. "It still stinks in here." He was right, the air was metallic on my tongue.

Two days earlier, Nick, the day shift clerk, was maced and robbed of the bank deposit. Someone wearing a motorcycle helmet, bike leathers, and gang colours came into the store, emptied two cans of pepper spray into Nick's face, and made themselves five thousand dollars richer. The only thing Nick knew about the thief was that it had been a woman.

"Tits, man, the bitch had really big tits," he told police.

"When's Nick coming back?" I asked Rob.

"Never. His wife threatened to kill him if he did."

"Amateur," Witt called from the counter. "Maybe we should send him a Get Well present."

"Penis enlargers are on sale," Rob suggested. We all laughed. It wasn't that we weren't sympathetic, but in two years the three of us had survived a clerk shot in the parking lot, two drug busts, ten armed robberies, four managers, and a fire set by a disgruntled employee. Maybe we *weren't* so sympathetic, after all.

ROB took my arm.

"Work upstairs tonight. And we need to talk." I followed him outside and up the steps. The sun was still high in the Caribbean-blue sky. Just another perfect day in that paradise town known as Phoenix. A girl in a passing car screamed, "Pervert!" The paint store guys shook their fists at us.

"What's up with them?" I asked. Rob sighed.

"Still washing down your Prozac with scotch?" he asked.

"Gin. And they're tranquilizers, not Prozac."

"Got any extra?"

"No."

"Selfish. Uh, MJ quit."

"I thought he loved this job. What happened?"

"Two guys and a 9mm." I nodded. That would explain the shell casings. Apparently, a gentleman of Anglo heritage was at the store around 3 A.M., perusing our fine selection of bondage materials. After making a sizable purchase, he returned to his Jeep Laredo in time to find another gentleman of undetermined origins about to abscond with said vehicle. Understandably concerned, the fellow took out a very large, fully automatic 9mm weapon and proceeded to spray the area. MJ, the janitor, who was on his way to the Dumpster with several bags of trash, dove into the oleanders as bullets whined past his ears. After reloading, the man continued to fire at the escaping felon-wannabe, hitting, among other things, the paint store across the street, taking out several cans of Dutch Boy Fresh & Easy on display in the front window. That explained the attitude from across the street.

"Where was security?" I asked, struggling to keep a straight face. Rob shot me a sidelong glance and then we erupted into laughter.

At times, we had needed protection from our protection. One guard conducted all his drug deals in the parking lot. Another followed female customers around, making lewd suggestions. Our current rent-a-cop was Tim, an eighteen-year-old vegetarian from Oregon with a shaved head and a ring in his nose. He liked to go up on the roof and throw pennies at parked cars.

The store began jumping around eight o'clock. We caught a guy eating body puddings and a woman trying to steal a Betty Page art book. A man buying magazines eyed me with appreciation.

"You ought to pose for them," he gushed, waving around a copy of *Plumpers,* a magazine that features naked fat women.

Witt called from the first floor to report that the Knock-Down Lingerie man was in the store.

Among the carnival of lost souls that blew through our doors was a collection of petty criminals, like the lingerie dude whose M.O. was to fill his arms with sexy underwear, saunter to the counter, and then turn and make a mad dash for the door, knocking down anyone or anything in his path. His appearance always lent a festive air to an evening, and since most of the lingerie we carried was ugly, I was glad to see it go.

On this particular evening, during his flight to freedom, he knocked a display of french ticklers into a group of Japanese businessmen contemplating a bulk purchase of Spanish Fly.

During a brief lull in the madness, Witt, Rob, and I met on the steps to share a cigarette.

"Sickos!" screamed someone in a passing car. Rob sighed. Witt scanned the night sky.

"Not even a full moon."

Phoenix in August is like Blanche du Bois, hot and crazy. It had been an unusually humid summer, with no end in sight. The air outside was so thick it was like trying to breathe underwater through a wool blanket. Inside, the refrigerated air just made everything feel clammy. Sensational murders were being reported daily, and rape, robbery, and gang violence had escalated to an alarming high. Armageddon was a day away and people were jumpy.

My insides were churning. Every customer was a potential robber or killer. I gulped down a couple of tranquilizers with a swig of warm Coke. Actually, it was a normal night. We were all just on edge because there had been back-to-back excessive violence. Normal violence we could handle.

When Tim came on at ten, Rob ordered him to stay close to me. Rob would work with Witt on the first floor. I began to relax. Two tranquilizers bubbling through my bloodstream helped.

Another of our troubled regulars approached the counter and handed me a dirt-encrusted note. I AM A DEF MUTE. GIV ME A DOLAR.

My milk of human kindness having long dried up, I handed back the note and, making sure I was enunciating clearly so he could read my lips, said: "Fuck you. Get a job."

I handed back the note and, making sure I was enunciating clearly so he could read my lips, said: "Fuck you. Get a job."

Eleven o'clock arrived, and with it, the third shift staff. Because third shift was even wilder than second, all three clerks were armed to the teeth. Harry had a sawed-off shotgun and mace. Fitz carried a .38, and Dave had his brother's .22 and a baseball bat with a spike driven through it. I called them the Testosterone Triplets.

I started to close out my register. Witt and Rob left. Fitz and Harry clocked in, then went on a snack run. Tim had disappeared. Dave chatted as I counted the drawer. The store was quiet.

"*Hey!*" screamed Dave. "*I've got a gun!*" He waved it for emphasis. I looked up to see a kid cramming videos into a laundry bag. He started to run, dragging the sack behind him. Dave raced to cut him off and tripped. The gun went off once, then twice. I heard a ZZZING! buzz by me. The kid dove through the door with Dave hot on his heels. I felt the familiar queasiness build in my guts and clutch my stomach. My hand came away wet. And bloody. I screamed. Nobody came to investigate the noise. I tore open my shirt and wiped away blood. There, like a mosquito bite, was a tiny pucker on my abdomen.

I had been shot.

What a stinking disappointment. No cops, bright television lights, sympathetic onlookers; no million-dollar settlement, just a torn shirt with a small bloodstain. It didn't even hurt. Much. Maybe that was because of the tranquilizers, too.

When I got outside, I found out why no one had come to my rescue. Tim, Fitz, and Harry were in the parking lot, laughing it up with a couple of working girls.

I never told anyone about the shooting. Dave would have ended up in jail and I couldn't do that to the guy. He deserved a chance to kill someone. As for me, I wasn't going to die with a dildo in my hand, at least not in public. So I quit. And two weeks later, I watched in relief as the Copper State disappeared from my rear view mirror.

Copper is the colour of blood, isn't it?

Stripper Manqué

IT'S BEEN YEARS SINCE I ESCAPED my hometown, now as then burdened with nonplussed citizens and limited job opportunities. Some blamed the heat, which attracted such exotic visitors as dragonflies (harmless), snakes (not so harmless), and palmetto bugs that would fly at you with the velocity of a box of Junior Mints being inhaled by a juvenile at a candy store. Others said the billboards – one for every brand of cigarette known to man – made the town feel crowded even when few people were on the streets. The giant, tanned blondes in the giant, peeling advertisements seemed to be the only people in town who were having any fun.

The ad people and the strippers, the countless dancers and "models" may have had their woes, but at least they weren't ascribing them to our town's lack of get-up-and-go.

It seemed a natural thing to stumble into one of these places, if only for entertainment value, since the strip clubs outnumbered our shopping malls and movie theatres four to one. One night when I was all dressed up with not one place to go after breaking up with a boy who wanted to move me to Alabama – Alabama! – I stuffed some cotton in my bra, put on comfortable shoes, and walked less than a mile to the nearest girlie joint.

Unfortunately, I was hired on the spot. A mastodon of a man aptly named T-Bone directed me to his office, which was only a slightly refurbished bathroom. Smoke jumped into my eyes, but I could still see ashes everywhere. When T asked me to pull up a chair, I sat on a sink.

After I showed T my identification, I assured him I wasn't a cop, just a lonely, bizarre twenty-year old who needed some fast cash. The T man wasn't convinced. Before I could ask for another office/bathroom to change in, Mr. T had my halter top down and my cotton balls went flying like loose change.

The boss was not pleased. He crossed his angry arms, shook his greasy head, and murmured, "Just tonight, hon."

This was before the days of body-beautiful feminism; Camille Paglia wasn't writing essays about power-hungry sex workers and Naomi Wolf wasn't around yet to introduce us to our inner Shakti.

I was wondering if I had slightly more sex appeal than lint when T escorted me to a narrow runway decorated with cigarette butts and sad little Christmas lights, a few of them actually blinking. As a new girl, I would be relegated to a side stage for the duration of my shift while the old pros – "hammers," as T-Bone lovingly referred to them – made all the money. One look at these Amazon women and I could see the girlie circuit was no place for me. To the chagrin of my employer I walked right up to the main stage, rotating like a cake display case, and checked out the mighty competition. One woman had blue scars on her face, another contusions all over her legs, but no matter. These women were huge, and in this world, bigger is always better.

I tripped over a football-shaped hairpiece, and ran screaming from what I assumed was a rat.

I tried to sashay back to my corner, but I tripped over a football-shaped hairpiece, and ran screaming from what I assumed was a rat. Champagne, a concerned table dancer, asked if someone had stolen a tip from me. She gave me twenty bucks just for pointing at the hairpiece.

I knew I wasn't missing my calling here, but still, something egged me on. I just wanted to see if I could do it. The answer: an unequivocal No.

When I finally got my close-up, I could only focus on the face of this one businessman who looked like he sold anthrax for a living. He was

the kind of guy who chewed toothpicks at places where no food was served. He was short and rotund with hair everywhere except on the top of his head. Maybe the hairpiece belonged to him. Of course he didn't tip a single dollar, and when Aretha Franklin's "R-E-S-P-E-C-T" hit the portable speakers, you could have cut the stage in half with the irony. To add insult to my travesty, I hadn't thought to bring stiletto heels, so I'm dancing in my bare feet like Salome, wondering whom I could bribe to bring me the bald, smirking head.

Finally, I couldn't take it anymore. I had been drinking martinis all night to rev up my courage, but now it was time to get even. I threw a fresh drink at the customer-from-hell's fuzzy face, and wasn't even surprised when he ate the olive that hit him in the eye.

In the end, I made twenty bucks, total, for shrieking at a toupee. I wanted to thank Champagne again for her much-needed contribution, but she was nowhere to be found. She had disappeared, and I didn't want to know where. I used the money for a taxi home, and left the driver a big tip.

A Born King of Something

Where do you live?

At the time I was mailing out call-up papers to reservists during the day and working nights behind the bar at a place called Schnapps. I had my own room in a hostel for soldiers just outside Tel Aviv. Towards the end of my first of three years in the army, I told the military shrink I was scared the other soldiers would beat me up in the showers, so she had me transferred to a base closer to home. That's when I moved into the hostel.

What do you have to offer our company?

I woke at 3 A.M. with Moshe's sharp little prick stabbing at the walls of my arse. I pushed myself up onto all fours and bit into my pillow. He came in my bum and then fell asleep beside me. I lay awake until morning. I watched him sleep on his back and wanted to put my head on his soft, hairy tummy. The following morning, over coffee made in a saucepan with a heating element, Moshe told me he ran a pub in Tel Aviv. That evening, I was learning to pour draught beer with a fine head. I worked at Schnapps with Moshe for the next sixteen months, seven nights a week.

What are your main skills and achievements?

I changed out of my uniform in the small kitchen by the bar. I left the curtains open while I dressed and let Moshe watch me from the counter while he spoke to his suppliers on the phone. Then I checked the oil in the deep fryer and made sure each table had a glass ashtray and Carlsberg coasters. I sliced cucumbers and tomatoes and washed a head of lettuce. I used these to decorate the toasted cheese platter which was served with chips and Syrian olives. Students from the ballet academy above the pub came to drink at the bar on their way home. When they were there I walked around as if my body had been shaped by a life's-worth of pliés, hoping one of the men would discover me and take me home. After work we went back to Moshe's and I sat on him until he came inside me. With him on his back I could manoeuvre his cock so it didn't crash into the walls of my arse.

What are your hobbies and interests?

The adjutant, Nimrod his name was, attacked me with a craft knife and pinned me to the wall behind my desk, saying: Beg. Come on, beg. Say you worship the ground I walk on. He was short and plump and recounted in detail how he'd shot a man during the war in Lebanon. His girlfriend objected to him working with me. With a poof, that is. Then there was the time crabs covered my body. I was given shampoo at the clinic but Nimrod made me wait until it was time to go home. He said he'd give me a lift back to Tel Aviv. We stopped off at his girlfriend's on the way. We stayed in the car and she leaned on his window while they talked about their wedding-to-be. He told her I was crawling with crabs. Then he drove me to Schnapps and said I should stop letting Moshe fuck me like a whore. He said he'd give me some money to pay the rent at the hostel if that's why I was doing it. That night I got rid of the crabs after Moshe had gone to sleep.

Have you any physical disability?

Simon – my boyfriend and best friend at the time – said that everyone knew big dicks hurt less than small ones. Simon had a very big cock. I never told him about Moshe. Simon was serving in a reconnaissance unit on the northern border and came to spend weekends at the hostel. While I was at work Friday and Saturday nights he'd watch TV in the communal living room downstairs. One Friday afternoon Moshe knocked on the door while Simon and I were in bed. We chatted for a while and then Moshe said he had to be going. He asked me to walk him to his car. We went up onto the roof and Moshe said he really needed to fuck me so I bent over the sink where the tenants did their hand-washing and let him poke around inside me. That evening Simon told me he was going to work in the fisheries in Alaska after the army. I still had fourteen months to go.

Please give details of any serious illness, operations
or accidents (with dates).

David Mendel has come to me in my dreams since nursery school. He is my true lover. When we were seven his Irish setter, Sean, chased me across the terra cotta patio by the pool. I escaped onto the table and fell through its glass surface. A triangular shard stuck in my arse-cheek. I said I couldn't feel a thing and that I didn't need a doctor. Couldn't I just stay and play and have the glass taken out later? His mother drove me to Emergency, where they stitched me up and then she took me home. Another time we went on holiday to Cape St. Francis where David's sister chased me down the corridor with a pair of scissors. I ran into the leg of an overturned chair and had four stitches sewn into the top of my foot by an Afrikaans doctor in Humansdorp. I sat up and watched the doctor inject me and then stitch up my flesh. I wasn't allowed onto the beach for the rest of the holiday.

Do you speak any foreign languages?

I was fourteen when my parents took me to Israel from South Africa. When I was first learning Hebrew I'd get confused and Afrikaans words would slip out like memories. Once I woke up next to Moshe and spoke to him in English. He looked at me and said: Do you realize what language you're speaking? I said I was sorry and translated what I'd just said into Hebrew. He said he'd understood perfectly well what I'd said the first time.

How do you get on with people?

I hoped I'd get to meet Moshe's flatmate. She was one of the only transsexuals in Tel Aviv. Moshe said she was the only one who wasn't a prostitute. She was a florist in a shop in the mall on Dizengoff Street. I wondered if Moshe had told her about me and whether it would be a nice idea to pop in and introduce myself next time I passed by the flower shop.

How do you cope with pressure?

I learned to love gin gimlets at Schnapps. I found the recipe for them in a book for bartenders under the counter. The book said they were popular amongst the colonials in Africa. I'd have my first one at ten, two hours before closing time. Moshe never let on if he knew I was drinking. I think the lime cordial took away the smell of the gin. Just like fresh lemon juice washes traces of garlic from your fingers. By the time we got home I was so drunk I'd sail up and down on him with my eyes closed until he grunted and came inside me. Sometimes I'd fall asleep before it was over and Moshe would have to catch me and lower me onto the bed so he could fuck me on my side. In the mornings I'd shower, put on my uniform, and take the bus to the base. My officer loved fresh croissants and, being on good terms with the cook, would smuggle a pot of cardamom coffee into the office each morning. We'd dip the croissants into our army-issued sky-blue plastic cups of coffee and make loud eating noises and laugh and Nimrod would say: When the fuck are you going to start working?

What do you hope to get out of the job?
Simon came back from Alaska after the first fishing season. He said he was cold and homesick. I had a month to go before my army duty was over. I got a job in the kitchen at the Senõr Sandwich sandwich bar on Ibn Gvirol Street. Simon started to introduce me to other gay men. Once we had an orgy and Simon said I was embarrassing him by asking everyone to fuck me.

Where would you like to be in five years time?
I want to stand up and tell stories to whole countries round a campfire. I'd like to have my own vegan café with big cushions and low tables and a menu that changes every day. I want to be loved and respected. I want to meet a man so huge I will be weak with adoration. I want to fuck death-white, skinny, hairless Englishmen and rip my nails across their backs. I want every memory to be present.

Do you have any questions?
I don't remember what happened to Moshe and why I stopped working at Schnapps. I stuck it out at Senõr Sandwich for a couple of months. I used to bring leftover sandwiches back to the hostel, having returned the slices of ham and cheese to the fridge, and share them with the Russian immigrant couple in the next room. At one point I started sleeping with the husband but then they got offered a flat in Haifa so I helped them pack and move. Simon and I drifted apart and recently I discovered he was having an affair with an ex of mine. He was always spiteful and resentful and never forgave me for leaving him. If I get this job I'm going to save up and go abroad for a while. Maybe for a couple of years. London, perhaps. A friend of mine told me it's no problem finding a job there if you're willing to do that kind of work.

Phone Sex Hell

"Who the gods would destroy they first make bored."

THERE WERE THIRTY OF US, all women, gasping and moaning into our receivers. Ginger, the woman at the desk to my right, was annoyingly loud, destroying my caller's carefully maintained illusion that I was sprawled on my bed, clad only in stockings and heels. I snapped my fingers at her, the agreed upon signal to keep it down. She made a face, lowering her voice for all of half a minute. Just another night in phone sex hell, I thought to myself. At three A.M., we were still getting calls from the drunks on the Western Seaboard, and now the early risers on the East Coast were beginning to check in. The burning question was whether the drunk at the other end of the phone would get his rocks off before I got a blister from sucking my little finger.

You have to understand that this was not a wholly awful job. The money was good. The shifts were flexible, a necessity for many of the artists and actors who worked at Cybervoice. We had breaks, a lunch room, and sympathetic managers. What eventually got to everyone was the tedium. These men paid five dollars a minute to talk with me. My phone persona, Jane, would do almost anything they asked but, apparently, ninety-five percent of these men lacked any sexual imagination. Inevitably, all they wanted was the same tired old fantasy: oral sex first, followed by vaginal sex from the rear, with a climactic finale of anal penetration. Come on, guys, this you can do in real life! These men must have all watched the same dumb pornos. And I would participate in at least fifty of these inane sexual dramas during every shift.

So how did a nice, thirty-plus, degree-holding woman like myself end up in this position? Employment opportunities in my field were scarcer than hen's teeth and, like Scarlett O'Hara, I had sworn, "Never again!" albeit in reference to bartending rather than to hunger. As I looked through the help wanted columns in the local paper, the phrase "good phone voice and lack of inhibitions" caught my eye. So did the promise of generous remuneration. Using my huskiest voice, I called in and was invited to come for an interview. For practice I called a chat-line (women call for free) and faked my way through a couple of audio orgasms. "No problem," I thought, heading down to the interview.

I, too, would soon be able to bring a man to orgasm while reading Ms. *magazine.*

I expected a sleazy massage parlour ambience, but the address proved to be a respectable office building in the downtown. The woman who met me at the door was pleasant and nicely dressed. We sat down in her office. "Say: fuck me harder!" she demanded. I nearly choked. She laughed, but continued, "Seriously, I need to know if you can talk dirty." I complied, ad-libbing a few moans and sighs for good measure. I was led into a nicely decorated room occupied by women of all ages and sizes. One woman was so heavily pregnant that her panting might well have been mistaken for the onset of labour. There were several butch lesbians, a few women in curlers, and some women incredible enough to be the stuff of my fantasies. No one wore lingerie; jeans and sneakers dominated. Several women read books while they gasped into the ears of their customers. I, too, would soon be able to bring a man to orgasm while reading *Ms.* magazine.

I was introduced to the floor manager and given a headset to listen in on live calls. This was to be my training. And yes, there was a distinctly voyeuristic thrill in listening in on the first few calls.

It was quickly apparent that this would be far from an electronic version of Anaïs Nin's intriguingly bizarre erotica. Directed to pick a name that would be my phone sex alias, I chose Jane, a play on "Plain Jane." After all, there was already a glut of Crystals, Natashas, and so on. I modelled Jane on Jane Seymour, an actor I despise. That long hair would come in handy, I thought. And so it did, wrapped tightly around thousands of imaginary (to me) penises. Jane wore tiny scraps of satin, played constantly with her nipples and clitoris, came about seven times an hour, and strapped on her giant dildo upon request. Jane was a virtual sex fiend, willing to indulge anything but pedophilia, bestiality, necrophilia, golden showers or scat, all prohibited by U.S. telecommunications regulations. Jane would dress you up in diapers and women's clothing and take you out to a biker bar. Jane loved to give head and get fucked up the ass. Of course she'd make it with her best friend in front of you! Jane was responsible for thousands of semen-drenched morsels of Kleenex.

Jane had fans, men who called her every night and wrote to the P.O. box that Cybervoice rented. I was paid extra for request calls and given three dollars for every letter that I replied to. We had albums full of pictures of women wearing lingerie and pouty expressions. I picked the one who looked the most like the imaginary Jane and, for ten dollars per photo, would send them on to these besotted fools. Jane even received a marriage proposal, and many of her letters included photographs of the men who thought that their ten-minute phone calls constituted a relationship. I was surprised by the ordinary good looks of most of these men. They weren't trolls. These were men who could have been dating and having sex with real, breathing, sweaty, attractive women.

At first, I liked the job. The novelty intrigued me – there was a certain cachet to telling my artistic friends about my life as an imaginary sex toy. The money was better than being a Starbucks barista and it didn't matter what I wore. The first annoyance was the flakes of skin forming on my little finger, the one I sucked on for appropriate sound effects. Then I began to dream of dreary sex with faceless, passive men. I didn't need to be Freud to understand these were work-inspired. And finally boredom, a crushing boredom, set in. We had to try and keep them on the phone a full ten minutes, which usually meant attempting a flirty chat for the first few minutes. Meanwhile, all they wanted was to come quickly and save money. I didn't want to prolong the conversation either, so I was frequently chastised by the phone monitor for going straight to the sex. I started to suggest ornate fantasies (bring on the dancing, cross-dressing dwarves) that scared them into hanging up. I gave them a hard time about their wives and girl-friends, often asleep in their bedrooms while the men called me, *sotto voce*, from living room phones.

On my last night there, I was pretending to whip a trick on the balls, the sound of my book hitting the desk simulating the noise, when I felt a wave of utter and acute tedium wash over me. The money was no longer worth it. I disengaged my head-set, picked up my coat, and left.

D E

S K

Corporate Me

THE WORST JOB I ever had was as a Credit Analyst at Data General Corporation. I was twenty-six years old and the company was catapulting up the curve of high-technology growth that was to last a surprisingly short amount of time. I got the job due to the recommendation of a co-worker who had a crush on me. I was a Clerk-Receptionist and he thought it would be better for the company if someone with my intelligence could be "better utilized."

The first day on the job my supervisor showed me a white telephone resting naked and silent on a desk in an unoccupied cubicle. He handed me a three-ring binder bulging with computer printouts. He pointed vaguely to the numbers and codes and told me that these were my customers. He explained that they all owed money to Data General. Some of them owed hundreds of thousands of dollars and others only a small amount. It was my job, my mission, to call all of these customers and get them to pay Data General the money they owed.

"Good luck," he said, and walked away.

I studied the computer printouts and painstakingly made sense of the customer codes, order numbers, sales prices, discounts, amounts paid and due. Sweat formed on my back and upper lip as I listened with increasing anxiety to the male voices cascading over my cubicle walls. Assertive, definitive, and undoubtedly all successful in collecting vast sums for the company.

I dreaded opening my mouth. I was convinced that my supervisor and several other male conspirators were huddled on the other side of the cubicle wall waiting gleefully for my plunge into corporate finance. I had been sitting there for over an hour without making one call. I started to panic. Frozen in air-conditioned sweat, I sat staring at the telephone. Finally, I came up with what felt like an excellent idea. I decided not to jump into the cavernous depths of credit collecting headfirst, but instead give myself a chance to "warm up."

Frozen in air-conditioned sweat, I sat staring at the telephone.

Energized, I scanned the computer sheets until I located a customer in Akron, Ohio who owed $15.95 for software that was over ninety days due. Dialing, I decided to ask for the name on the printout. I was put through to Jim Anderson's office where I declared I was calling from Data General Corporation. I told him my name and that I was calling to collect the funds owed on invoice number 592735 for software. A long pause. He asked me the amount of the bill. I told him. Another long pause. Then he started screaming like a lunatic.

"We have twenty of your goddamned computers lined up in our testing area and I can't get any of them to work. I have shipping deadlines to my customers!" Then his voice increased considerably in volume and emotion. *"We're talking about a couple of million dollars worth of computer equipment just sitting on my dock and you're calling me about a bill for fifteen dollars! What are you? A moron?"*

AND HE HUNG up the phone.

I sat there listening to the buzz for quite a while and then, for the sake of my supervisor and the men who must still be listening on the other side of the cubicle wall, I had the aplomb to speak into the dead telephone line, "Yes, sir. I understand. I will call back. Thank you."

EVE CORBEL

Accounting-Clerk Secretary
To the Devil

HI, I'M EVE CORBEL, AND I THINK I'M OKAY NOW BUT FOR A YEAR OF MY LIFE, I WAS **ACCOUNTING CLERK-SECRETARY** to the **DEVIL**

IT WAS A GOOD-PAYING UNION JOB IN A SMALL COLLEGE BOOKSTORE

A CALM-LOOKING PLACE WITH REAL LIGHT & AIR.

MY WORKMATES WERE QUITE COOL. (EXCEPT FOR BERNARD J. WEYMOUTH,

MEG CASHIER/CLERK ↑ REALLY SWEET

RALPHIE STOCKBOY/GOPHER ↑ SO CALM

THE STORE MANAGER)

AND THE WORK WASN'T TOO SCARY. (USUALLY.)

RECONCILING DELIVERY SLIPS AND INVOICES

FILING

BOOKKEEPING

CASHING OUT

EVE! TAKE A LETTER TO THE SCHOOL BOARD... RE: YOURS OF 27TH, I CONCUR ...DISCREPANCIES IN STOCK.. MAJOR SHOPLIFTING PROBLEM. SOPHISTICATED METHODS ...FOREIGN STUDENTS... blah bl...

REGISTRATION DAY

EVE! GET OUT ON THE FLOOR AND WATCH FOR **THIEVES!** I'LL TAKE OVER YOUR CASH!!

THANK YOU... NEXT! MOVE ALONG!

WHY ISN'T HE RINGING IN THOSE SALES?

YOU'D BETTER DO AN INTERIM DEPOSIT. TOO MUCH CASH ON HAND, IN FULL VIEW OF **ALL THESE STUDENTS!!**

B. WEY!

720, 740, 760, 780, 800, 820, 84

HUH??!!

I.O.U. $30

WHAT'S THIS, MEG?

SOMETIMES MR. WEYMOUTH BORROWS CASH AND LEAVES A CHIT.

FOR HOW LONG DOES HE BORROW IT?

OH... A MONTH OR TWO.

OR A BIT LONGER.

LATER THAT DAY...

WHEW! WHAT A DAY!

I'LL CASH OUT TONIGHT. YOU GO ON HOME.

ARE YOU SURE?

OF COURSE. GO AHEAD.

NEXT MORNING...

WELL DONE, STAFF! THE CASH BALANCED TO THE PENNY LAST NIGHT!!

WHAT ABOUT THE CASH HE NEVER RANG IN?

OH BOY! BERNARD ORDERED THE NEW AUSTEN EDITIONS! I'M GONNA BUY A FEW OF THEM.

YOU SHOULD BUY THEM NOW, EVE. THEY'LL GO REAL FAST.

OKAY— I'LL DO IT AT LUNCH.

THEY'LL BE GONE BY THEN.

HEY!! THERE'S ONLY **TWO LEFT!!**

WHO BOUGHT THEM ALL?!

TIK TIK TIK TIK

NO ONE BOUGHT ANY OF THOSE BOOKS.

BUT--

ONE MONTH LATER...

CLOSED FOR INVENTORY

3 AT 15.95, 10 AT 9.95, 5 – NO, 4 – AT 14.95, 6 MORE AT 9.95, AT 89

THE COUNT WAS WAY, WAY UNDER, EVE! I AM **VERY UNHAPPY** WITH THE JOB YOU DID!!

BUT-- DON'T YOU GET IT? THE SCHOOL BOARD IS TRYING TO GET ME AND **YOU** HAVE GIVEN THEM THE MEANS!!

A MONTH AFTER THAT....

CLOSED FOR INVENTORY

4 AT 12.95, 1 AT 19.95, ARE THE AUDITORS STILL WATCHING? 3 AT 11.95, 2

YES

AND A MONTH AFTER THAT...

YOU **IDIOTS!** CAN'T EVEN DO INVENTORY! GET OUT!! YOU'RE **ALL FIRED!**

DON'T WORRY, EVE. HE'LL CALL US BACK TOMORROW.

CAMILLA GIBB

That's PhD to You

THE LAST TIME A JOB VACANCY was posted in my discipline at the University of Toronto was in 1981. I was twelve. Sixteen years later I find myself returning home with a PhD from Oxford less than optimistic about my job prospects. I read, with a mixture of relief and despair, statistics which state that the average age of first full-time employment in academia today is thirty-six. I take this as partial reassurance that it's not me, but I am aware that I am not as academically hungry as I need to be. I am, however, starting to get hungry – I am unemployed and losing sleep over the next impending nine years of student loan repayments.

Fear compels me to take a job as a Career Placement Officer. I am licking more envelopes and making less money than in the year I worked as a secretary before going to graduate school, but a certain degree of detachment allows me to see the irony of the situation. My particular clients are people who have or are expecting their PhDs and one of the "challenges" outlined in my job description is "tactfully suggesting alternatives to academic employment." But I have difficulty containing my cynicism. I want to look across the counter at these graduate students and tell them: "This is what your PhD will get you. You too could be a Career Placement Officer."

Your PhD apparently gives you "transferrable skills" in the areas of research, writing, and communication. In the non-academic world these skills might, for instance, enable you to compose generic, formulaic letters, qualify you to answer a phone, or ensure that you rapidly acquire the technical jargon relevant to any new working environment. That is, of course, if anyone will hire you. You have, after all, very little real-world work experience, save for that odd assortment of summer and part-time jobs, and with a PhD, well, you probably have an "attitude" or "expectations." God forbid, you might even have the audacity to occasionally interject, "Actually, that's Dr., not Miss."

Here, in the world of careers, the opposite of "good news" is known as *"other* realistic news." Other realistic news in academia refers, among other things, to the fact that less than three percent of faculty in Canada are under the age of thirty-six. Among my contemporaries, we share testimonials about this "other" reality. Steven, who I meet in my first bout of envelope licking, has a PhD in English. He tells me that the average academic opening in his discipline attracts anywhere between 500 and 1,200 applicants. He, like many others, has started to apply to lesser-known colleges in the rural wastelands of obscure American states. His last attempt, however, was returned unopened, with a note stating that with 450 dossiers received well in advance of the May 1 deadline, the department could not hope to process any more applications. My last was to Northwestern for a junior faculty position – a posting which attracted more than 800 applications.

On Day Three of my new career, I attend a workshop for students and recent graduates offered by the employment service entitled "Identifying Skills and Options." It is interactive, and involves sorting through a lot of colour-coded cards with pictures and adjectives on them, classifying yourself as a personality type, looking at the overlap between your skills and interests, and identifying your values.

Values is where I start to lose it. I have already had plastic-colour-coded-card confirmation that I am a virtual anarchist and by this last stage I am being told that if I do not find an ethically sympathetic environment in which to work, I will be discontented and unhappy. Ironically, my employer is helping me to uncover the evidence which will ultimately empower me to quit.

Here I am sitting in on my second workshop reading over a sheet of tips on successful networking, the key to accessing the unadvertised job market. Networking demands constant awareness that everyone you meet is a potential contact and perpetual self-assessment on these terms. The tip sheet helpfully suggests not smoking or drinking excessively at parties for this reason.

I am beginning to feel nostalgic for our departmental seminars at the Gardener's Arms in north Oxford, where a near century of anthropologists have simultaneously taxed their livers and brains. It's not the alcohol – it's the intensity, the passion, the tenured guarantee of academic freedom, the thinking, the discussion, the idiosyncrasies which seem squashed by the networking suggestions in front of me.

This is not a place where many of us can say, "this is what I expected to be when I grew up"

This is a different world. Here I am presented, on my third day, with the challenge of an "unstructured," "unsupervised" half-hour during which my resourcefulness is tested and observed. I am wistful and reminiscent – remembering the year and a half of "unsupervised" solitary fieldwork in a Muslim village in the highlands of Eastern Ethiopia, remembering the "unstructured" moments of creative insights drafted in the wee hours of the morning.

Toward the end of the week I am presented with an even bigger challenge. Would I like to "try drafting a letter?" I have written a 100,000-word thesis. I have academic publications because I have been warned all my life that if I don't, I will perish. I am editing a book. But I am paralyzed. Tears are welling up in my eyes as I gaze at the computer screen.

All week I have been the recipient of mini-sermons on how to deal with identified "types" of people. There are people with PhDs – these are people who are unrealistic and idealistic and given to arguing about the economy more than trying to engage in it. And there are Generation Xers. These are people who are "unwilling to pay their dues." Having a PhD and being of said generation, I find it particularly challenging to heave myself over the fence onto more objective ground. I am finding it hard to look into the faces of my contemporaries who are staring at me blankly saying, "I need a job. Any job. I don't care."

My position demands that I recognize evidence of "teachable moments." I am encouraged to respond to visible displays of uncertainty, hesitation, lack of confidence or direction by asking people if they have thoroughly assessed their skills and interests and explored their options. "And do you know what type of work you are looking for?" I might ask as someone stares at me thinking "Duh, the kind that pays." And I might proceed by saying, "We really encourage people to attend this interactive workshop. . . ." when I know that they just want to bulldoze their way past my counter to the job listings.

For many people, the workshops are undoubtedly helpful. They offer some suggestions for approaching what otherwise presents itself as an overwhelming and daunting job market, help one realize one's marketability, and probably do go some way toward engendering optimism in those of us who are less cynical. But when I hear, "I had a sessional contract at Trent which just ended and I'm desperate. I'm prepared to do anything, to wait tables," I am reminded that not many of us have the privilege of thinking in terms of skills and interests and what is relevant to our degree.

This is not a place where many of us can say, "this is what I expected to be when I grew up" – a telemarketer, a waiter, a fund-raiser, a bicycle courier, or a "temp." This is not a place in which we really entertain the notion of "career." An earlier generation saw a direct, linear relationship between education and employment, and work was about salary and status which increased incrementally as one moved up the ladder.

We don't move that way now. We cobble together a patchwork of opportunities and experiences and are grateful when some of them pay. Like most people I know, I find myself responding to the cringe-worthy question of "what do you do?" with "do you mean what do I do for money or what do I really do?"

The difficulty is that the time and energy required to establish yourself as a young academic virtually precludes doing much else to make money. One cannot at this stage be a part-time academic, and making money outside does nothing to enhance an academic c.v. The journey is increasingly one of sessional contracts with excessive teaching responsibilities for stipend pay throughout the wastelands of the North American interior. In terms of a "life" I find myself wondering if it can possibly be worth it. A week as a Career Placement Officer, however, tells me that I have little other choice.

My week (and my new "career") ends after a brief conversation with one of the Career Counsellors. He has read about me in the SuperMemo which circulates around the office and approaches me sympathetically. "This must be really hard for you."

I manage to maintain the near cultish grin of optimism which is mandatory office dress here and object, "Oh no. It's good. There's a lot to learn."

"Most people with PhDs wouldn't be able to swallow their pride like this," he says. He is trying to be supportive. It is Friday at five minutes to five. I look back over what I have learned this week and present my case for quitting in exactly the language given to me by my employer. If I have learned anything as a Career Placement Officer, it is how to quit a job convincingly.

Death Would Be a Welcomed Visitor

"PURPLE IS MY POWER COLOUR," June, the executive director, said. It was my first day of work and I had complimented her on her suit. The suit was black. It was her blouse that was purple. "I always wear a bit of purple. And on days when I need an extra power boost, I wear more." Other people take vitamins, I thought to myself. "You know, Laura, purple has a very important significance to our work here."

"How is that?" I inquired.

"You see, the colour purple was originally derived from menstrual blood. And as you know, life is nurtured on menstrual blood. And that's what we do here. We raise money to enable our good doctors and nurses to carry on their important work in the healing arts. Money, you see, is our menstrual blood."

Martha, the assistant director, sauntered over to us and stood next to June. She turned to me, nodding her head, which was topped with short, tight red curls. "It's true," she said. "Purple is my favorite colour too."

"Martha, why don't you show Laura around the office? This afternoon I'll show her the mind map."

"Yes," said Martha, "the mind map." Then they hugged for what seemed to be a good five minutes. Martha had tears in her eyes. "I've been searching all my life for a mentor," Martha told me. "And now I've found her."

June held out her arms to me. "Welcome," she said. As she held me against her full, moist body, I caught the eyes of my new co-workers, Sally and Eliza. They smiled sympathetically and mouthed the word "lunch." I knew I had found allies, and it frightened me that I needed them.

Sally was plain, had a dry wit, and called things the way she saw them. Eliza was more flamboyant. Her favourite expression was, "Death would be a welcomed visitor." She wore flowing dresses in floral prints and ate nothing but sweets. I witnessed her emptying thirteen sugar packets into her coffee; she claimed it was only twelve. Eliza went to a psychiatrist in order to keep her Valium prescription. She said his specialty was in-patient care, but he took her on as a special case.

I witnessed her emptying thirteen sugar packets into her coffee; she claimed it was only twelve.

Over the next several months the us/them contingents were firmly established. June and Martha made up systems aimed at improving our fundraising ability while cutting costs. The systems were far too complex to be of any use, but we learned not to question or else listen to Martha's hour-long diatribe, the subtext of which asked the question: "Why are you so stupid?" Instead, we talked about them and their systems behind their backs.

June spoke openly of her dysfunctional origins and her wild past. She was now born again into some new age religion called the Rainbow Church. She shared with us the most intimate details of her life while we cringed in embarrassment. She attended seminars to open up her inner child and came back to the office filled with ideas on how to work together more harmoniously. She felt her role as director was to empower us, especially Eliza. From time to time June would call Eliza into her office for an inspirational chat, advising her on the power of positive thinking and trust in the universe. After hours behind closed doors, Eliza would emerge pale-faced and shaking. "I desperately need a cigarette," she'd say.

At a rainy Monday morning staff meeting, Eliza and I were talking about an impending storm. Eliza said she wouldn't be at work the next day if there was a blackout. "I can't put on makeup in the dark and I just won't go out without it," she said, opening another sugar packet. "Will you be able to come in tomorrow, Martha?" asked Eliza. "Being that you live on that big hill and all."

"I'll be here," Martha said, leaning back in her chair. She wore a wrinkled, faded green dress with a tear down the seam; the sole was coming off her shoe. "I have higher priorities than to worry about makeup."

June took Martha's cue. "Speaking of priorities, Martha, why don't you tell our colleagues about the new file system?"

"Information is key in our business," Martha announced. "And even though we live in the age of technology, the paper files are still, at a fundamental level, the tools to our ability to access the information we need. It is important that you understand this concept." Eliza and I smiled our assurance. Sally stared at her stone-faced.

"Good," she said, turning away from Sally's gaze. "June and I are very proud of this system," she bellowed. "We worked on it until after midnight Friday. Fundamentally, the principle behind the system is that colours will help us find the files we are looking for more efficiently when the file colour reflects the category the file falls into by playing upon our subconscious symbol system. For example – " She held up a black file folder. "The black files. These are potential donors who are unknown to us, or we are unknown to them. Black is the colour of the great unknown. Do you understand?"

Sally raised her hand. "Excuse me," she said, "but aren't those files more expensive then the manila ones?"

"Yeah," said Martha. "Isn't our ability to do our jobs in the most efficient manner worth the extra expense?"

"Death would be a welcomed visitor," Eliza whispered to me.

"What did you say, Eliza?" June asked. With a sudden motion, she reached across the table, taking Eliza's hands between hers. "What's wrong, Eliza?" she asked pleadingly. "Are you having problems at home? Please, please, share your troubles with us. We only have your peace and happiness in mind." Eliza was silent, stiff. "Trust me. We know, we understand. You are so fragile. We know."

Sally and I looked at each other, trying to figure out how to save our friend. Martha rolled her eyes. Eliza snatched back her hand from June's grip and walked out. We knew she was headed in the direction of the butt hut, her place of refuge.

June stood up flustered. For a moment it looked like she would go after Eliza.

"I haven't finished explaining the system," Martha said. June's face was bright red.

"Oh yes. Yes. Go ahead, Martha. Continue."

As Martha's voice droned on like white noise, Sally and I thought of Eliza shivering in the butt hut, smoking cigarette after cigarette, wiping June's sweat off the palm of her hand.

F E

E D

Feeding the Dreadfuls

IT SEEMED LIKE A typical Saturday night at Albert Wong's Pagoda. It was graduation weekend at the university. This would be the busiest night of the month. Graduates would be stopping in at Albert Wong's for that last order of Pagoda Lo Mein before leaving town for good. God, I thought wistfully, their last night at Albert Wong's.

I arrived at 6 and Albert, the owner of the restaurant, was sitting at his usual table cleaning his ear with a toothpick. I waved at him and grabbed a pen and a book of guest checks from the cashier's stand. I mouthed the words, "You're gonna go deaf."

"What?" He removed the toothpick for a second. Then he gave me the bad news. "Party of three in section 2."

I saw the Dreadfuls nestling into the brown vinyl seats. Mr. and Mrs. in the booth facing me, their son out of sight on the other side. He bobbed suddenly and I caught a glimpse of that hateful crown of red hair.

The other waitresses were snickering behind the bar.

"Bad karma," said Cheri, wagging her head like Eeyore.

Peggy grinned at me. She had one hazel eye and one blue eye and lots of freckles, so it was hard to know where to focus when you looked at her.

"Better you than me," she said. "Albert knows I want to kill that kid." Peggy had two cigarettes burning in the ashtray and was compulsively wiping down the liquor bottles. She was a whippet – thin, fast, and full of nervous energy. By contrast, Cheri barely seemed to be breathing. She was slow, so slow that she was a decade behind the rest of us. She played folk music in bars around town, and wore peasant blouses and earrings made from feathers.

"I better water 'em," I said. I got three glasses of ice water from the kitchen and approached the Dreadfuls' booth.

"Hello. How are you tonight?" The man and woman looked relieved to see another adult. The boy immediately started stirring his water with his spoon, spilling it on the rubbery red tablecloth. At least the tablecloth is indestructible, I thought.

"We're fine, thanks. Honey, say hello to the waitress."

The boy floated three ice cubes in his spoon and then flung them at me. The parents exchanged a complicated look of fear and resignation that they'd obviously been perfecting over the last six years. The mother's forehead seemed to wilt with anxiety. The father chewed a stubby fingernail. Seconds of silence passed before the father spoke.

"Jonathan, that was impolite," he reprimanded in a quiet, wavering voice.

"It's only water," I said because I felt sorry for them, but I gave the boy my needle eyes. He ignored all of us.

"What would you like to eat, Jonathan?" The mother took over to let the father recover from disciplining.

"I want a hamburger." He poked at the tablecloth with his fork.

"This is a Chinese restaurant. They don't sell hamburgers here. How about some nice fried rice?"

Oh, no, I thought. Not this routine, not tonight. The kid knows damn well where he is and what he's having for dinner: the same thing he orders every month when he comes in here and runs up and down our spines for two hours. I had to nip this in the bud.

"Okay, that's one pork fried rice. And two orders of Moo Goo Gai Pan, right?" The parents looked at me with a filmy expression of gratitude.

"I hate fried rice!"

I didn't give the parents a chance to respond. I leaned closer to the boy's ear and said, "It's special fried rice tonight. You're gonna love it."

I put their order in and went back into the dining room. Peggy was behind the bar rattling the ice around with a metal scoop. She seemed more keyed up than usual.

"Where's Albert?" she asked. "People are waiting for tables."

"I don't know. Where's Cheri? Her section's full."

"I don't know, but she sat the flirty psychology T.A. in your section."

I glanced around and saw the back of his head. "Is his girlfriend with him?"

"Nope. He's alone."

"Will you take him? Please? He tips well."

"Cheri said he specifically asked for you." Peggy was filling glasses with ice and then emptying them as if practicing for a test.

"What do you mean? He doesn't know my name."

"He described you." She smiled at me.

"He did? How?"

"He asked for the skinny waitress with the bad haircut."

"Well, that could be you."

Peggy stopped scooping ice. Her gaze went from my eyes to my hairline. "He meant you." She sounded mad.

I walked away rolling my eyes. It was time to feed the tyrant. I picked up the Dreadfuls' food and removed the lid from the boy's fried rice. I dusted his meal with hot mustard powder.

The Dreadfuls were pressed together, holding hands, as if trying to merge into one person with a decent backbone. The boy had managed to bore a hole in the tablecloth. Congratulations, I thought, a cigarette couldn't even do that.

"Here we are." I set the serving dishes down and removed the lids. "Moo Goo Gai Pan, Moo Goo Gai Pan, and Pork Fried Rice."

"I told you I hate fried rice!" The boy gave me a nasty look.

"I told you you're gonna love it because it's *special*," I said.

WITHOUT breaking eye contact, the boy took a handful of rice and threw it on the floor. My future flashed before my eyes: me at 11:00 that night, on my hands and knees, picking up grains of rice the vacuum cleaner rejected. The tyrant's rice!

Suddenly, he slipped like a fish off the booth and vanished under the table. I held up my hands to the parents as if to say, "Relax, let me handle this." I squatted and popped my head under the tablecloth. The boy was sitting cross-legged, staring straight ahead with his chin in his hands.

"You are being icky," I said quietly. "If you don't sit still and eat your dinner neatly, I'm going to banish you to section 3. There are lots and lots of cockroaches in section 3. They lay their eggs on the tape stuck to the back of those pictures, and when the babies hatch they swarm out by the hundreds and scamper into

"You are being icky," I said quietly.

your food. They do the backstroke in your hot and sour soup. They hop on your eggroll like it was a teeter-totter. They play King of the Hill on your fried rice. Is that where you want to eat your dinner?" He looked at me, but didn't answer. I hissed, "Is it?" I slowly removed my hands from the pocket of my apron in what I hoped was a threatening gesture. He slid back up the seat. He looked at his dinner, picked up his fork, and then looked back at me. Mr. and Mrs. Dreadful picked up their forks and looked at me, too. I nodded my approval.

"Enjoy your dinner," I said, backing away from the table. Before I got to the kitchen, I heard a shriek from the dining room and then a child crying. I pushed through the swinging kitchen door, took an eggroll from the warming pan, and wrapped it in a napkin. I grabbed my civilian clothes and a bottle of plum wine from the pantry. On my way out, I gave the wine to the Dreadfuls. I could almost see the moisture evaporating from their four eyes as they sat not blinking while the tyrant sobbed.

"Plum wine, courtesy of Albert. He's going to be your waitress tonight." I draped my apron over the cash register and ran out the door. Outside, I peeked in the window. In a few minutes, Albert came back into the dining room. I ate my eggroll and watched him look for me. Soon, he found my apron lying in my tracks like a discarded shell. I could see his mouth working, but couldn't hear him. Eventually, he put my apron on and went to work. I finished my eggroll, my last meal at Albert Wong's Pagoda.

32 Flavours

"WHAT FLAVOURS do you have?" This question posed as the man in the ugly cardigan stands below the sign that lists all thirty-two flavours of ice-cream. A scream wells inside the clerk but she stifles it and begins: "Black Cherry, Choklit Bomber, Lemon Sherbet, Icy Mint Fudge, Smoking Gun, Dripping Dagger, Smashed Skull, Pureed Cranium . . ."

The man in the cardigan turns pale. He is a Customer. He is frightened by the girl behind the counter of 32 Flavours. She *seems* normal: pony-tail, red lips, nice tits. But she is odd, and what she says is definitely bizarre and almost . . . *violent*.

"Excuse me?" the man asks, completely indignant. He can't believe this girl would really be so rude to a Customer.

"Chocolate Asshole, Severed Head Surprise, Death Valley Swirl, Bye-Bye Bastard Custard —"

"You're *sick!*" snaps the man. He quickly puts his money back into his wallet and storms out of the air-conditioned cool of the 32 Flavours. On the sidewalk, collecting his wits, he vows to call the Manager on Monday morning to complain. He might very well contact the 32 Flavours Head Office and demand an apology and gift certificate. By fax and by phone he will make sure that the girl is fired. All he had wanted was a little ice-cream cone and he had received this . . . *anger* instead. This unwarranted, perverse anger.

THE GIRL wipes the sticky counter with a warm wet cloth. She smiles to herself and changes the water in the bucket where the scoops are kept. Kept wet to make the scooping easier. She knows what a joke that concept is. Even if the scoops are heated to 400°F, the ice-cream still won't budge from the rock-hard paper tubs. It is either dripping all over everything or it has to be blasted out with a hammer and chisel. She hates scooping ice-cream for a living. It aggravates her and makes her think violent thoughts. She is convinced that most serial killers have at one time in their lives been food-service workers. It would explain a lot. The sticky gumminess that coats her arms from her finger-tips to her armpits gets on her nerves. Once she actually found a piece of cookie from Kooky Kookie lodged in her underarm. It disgusted her, all of it, but it is her job. She is poorly paid but, like thousands of other retail employees, her self-esteem has been shot to shit by the management practices of 32 Flavours and she is afraid to quit. There aren't too many jobs out there, she is lucky to even *have* a job. Chanting about Hard Times is the Manager's favourite way to crush her dream of ever quitting.

SHE DECIDES one afternoon that the next idiot who orders Bubblegum ice-cream and wears his baseball cap backwards will really get it. The full blast of her building rage. There is a big red callous on her thumb from digging into flavours like that, the ones filled with obstructions: Candy Cane, Crunchy Crunch, Bubblegum. On busy afternoons the callous bleeds, soaking the rag she wraps around the scoop handle to increase traction. Picking sugar from the split ends of her pony-tail, she fantasizes that it is December. Summer is hell at 32 Flavours. In December she can read books and daydream, and hardly anyone but the odd freak bothers her. In winter the shifts are shorter and her hands don't hurt as much. She doesn't feel quite as angry in the winter.

The gelati flavours are kept in an upright display freezer behind her. Sometimes, whirling around to yank the doors open, she sees herself reflected in the glass. A quick, blurry, horror-movie of a girl with a blunt silver object in one hand and a sugar cone in the other. There she is: a true-crime reading, ice-cream scooping, angry young woman.

She has a boyfriend, of sorts. He skis all winter and sails all summer. He is an absentee boyfriend. It works for her, and fulfills her mother's expectations. She has a friend, Wendy Carmichael, who comes by the store to visit with a Thermos full of Margaritas. Wendy feels sorry for the girl, and brings the drinks to soothe her frazzled nerves. After a few belts of Margarita, Wendy takes the girl into the back freezer and kisses her. They kiss until the next horde of ice-cream licking pigs marches in. The girl doesn't have time to question why she loathes her boyfriend and keeps kissing Wendy back. It's July. The bastards want their ice-cream.

She is convinced that most serial killers have at one time in their lives been food-service workers. It would explain a lot.

She hits the jack-pot one day: a creepy engineering student comes in with his frat-hat on backwards. It's cherry-coloured corduroy. He is leering, strutting, doing her a favour by smiling at her. Pretending to be boyish and innocent, a lad in search of a nice ice-cream cone to molest with his beer-soaked tongue.

He shuffles his feet, pretends he is bashful. He orders Bubblegum ice-cream. She snaps.

WENDY comes in that night with her Thermos. The 32 Flavours is quiet, an odd thing for a Saturday night in July.

The girl is nowhere to be seen behind the counter. The fridges hum, the air-conditioning is on too high. It's all normal, all the same except for the lack of Customers. Wendy looks down the hall that leads to the walk-in freezer at the back of the store. Seeing no sign of her friend, she sits down at one of the little purple tables and waits.

When the girl finally emerges from the back room she is smiling.

She wears a look of satisfaction Wendy has never seen before. It makes Wendy uneasy.

"Hi Wen!" The girl is positively singing. She begins wiping down all the counters, whistling a tune. When she looks up at Wendy, Wendy is staring down the hall that leads to the walk-in.

"Is there someone else here?" Wendy asks, trying to sound casual. After all, the girl has every right to entertain whomever she pleases in the walk-in freezer of the 32 Flavours.

"Of course not," the girl says brightly.

"Well . . . you seem kind of . . . uhmm . . . happy. It's weird."

The girl nods and smiles. "I've discovered the secret to enjoying my job. I read a book last night, *Do What You Love, Love What You Do, Too*. It talks a lot about anger and how it can ruin your job and your life if you let it. If you don't find a way to *channel* it. I've channeled! I'm thinking I might even buy a 32 Flavours franchise someday."

"What?" Wendy gasps.

"I am in control of my work experience. I have one life. I have to make the most of it. There are benefits to this job that I wasn't able to recognize before. I have taken control of my work experience tonight. Let me show you. . . ." She takes Wendy's hand and leads her toward the walk-in freezer.

"Hang on a sec!" Not even Wendy's amorous excitement can make her leave her Thermos behind on the table.

It is the first time that the girl is taking the initiative and is leading the way to the freezer. She doesn't seem drunk or high. It is a sober decision and one that makes Wendy's heart swoon. Before she opens the freezer door she gives Wendy a long and wonderful look. There is a new spark in the girl's eyes. Wendy leans forward and kisses her impulsively. The girl loosens her pony-tail and shakes her hair free.

"I hate scooping ice-cream, Wendy. I can't tell you the kind of rage that builds inside me after an hour or two of scraping at those buckets. The sickly-sweet smell, the air-conditioning. I've had a cold for three and a half years! It eats away at a person. Tonight I embraced the rage."

"You finally told a Customer to fuck off, didn't you?" Wendy squeals. "Way to go! They're all so rude to you, the pigs! Making you recite the flavours, all thirty-two!"

"That isn't what happened," the girl begins, but the bells on the front door clatter and she has to go out front. Wendy waits in the hallway with her Thermos, listening.

A family of three stands impatiently in the store, craning their necks as though they have been waiting there for several weeks instead of the few seconds that have passed. The girl appears, smiling. She offers each member of the family a free sample. The three of them smack their lips and make some of the most offensive noises the girl has ever heard. The ratty-wigged wife orders Low Fat Berry and then waves it away when the girl tries to hand it to her over the counter.

"Too runny," she whines. "Gimme Choklit Bunny!"

The husband snorts, "From Low Fat to So Fat!"

He stands and scratches his red beard, gazing up at the flavour list with matching red eyes. He ponders and sighs. The girl feels her old agitation building. She looks down at the little boy and he begins to bellow his order out but is silenced by a slap from his father.

"Daddy first!" the well-trained wife screeches between slurps of her cone.

"Hmmm. Uh. Let me see now. Thirty-two flavours, eh? It's hard to know."

"Lemon?" the wife suggests.

"*Shut up!*" he roars.

There is silence now, nothing but the whir of the freezers, the fan, the metallic wheezings of the air-conditioner.

"Sir?" the girl prompts.

"Just a goddamn minute!" the man snaps. He glares over the napkin dispenser at her.

"Daaaad!" the little boy whines.

"Gaaary, please!" the wife chimes.

The husband puffs up his chest and purses his lips into a thin, mean line. Slowly he raises one hair-coated arm and points to the door. "Do you want to go to the *car?*" he threatens his family.

The wife and little boy shake their heads and shrink down, waiting. The man turns back to the list of flavours. The girl hears the sound of the walk-in freezer door opening and her heart begins to pound. Wendy.

"Which one do *you* like?" the man asks, staring at the girl's breasts through the display case windows.

The girl's face goes hot with rage and she says quietly, "I'm vegan."

"WHAT?" the man shouts, leaning far over the counter, as far as he can manage.

"I'm waiting," the girl answers, stepping back from his sweating face.

"I'll have . . ." he licks his beefy lips, "I think I'll have . . . vanilla. *Vanilla.* S'at okay with you?"

The girl calls out to Wendy. She is hanging by her last nerve-ending. Wendy comes out from the back freezer with an ice-cream scoop in her hand.

"What'd he order?" she demands.

"After several moments of deliberation: vanilla," the girl whispers.

She snaps. Wendy snaps with her. The scoops fly and dagger.

WENDY and the girl sit in the walk-in freezer with the Thermos of Margaritas. They watch the little boy gleefully eating an entire tub of Banana Cloud. His legs are tied up but his arms are free.

"What was it that got you the first time?" Wendy asks.

"Bubblegum."

"I can see how that would do it. Plus the hat. The hat is a definite agitator."

The two girls look over at the place on the freezer floor where they have piled the bodies of the frat boy, the wife and red-bearded husband.

The bodies are stiffening in the cold of the freezer. They have spared the little boy, being optimistic at the bottom of their souls. It isn't the little boy's fault that his parents were Bad Customers.

"Are you going to quit?" Wendy asks.

The girl swigs Margarita and lets it splash down the front of her. Other splashes on her t-shirt have begun to freeze. She feels reckless and wild. Free.

"Well, my boss is on vacation. And we just had inspection. I'm running the place for another couple weeks at least. I think I should stick around."

"I think you should hire me!" Wendy exclaims.

"Well, I will need help," the girl nods. "There are still twenty-nine flavours to go!"

At this the girls howl, clinking their bloodied scoops together.

"How's your Banana Cloud?" Wendy asks the little boy.

"Very good, thank-you!" he answers, his mouth full.

"You're on the right road," the girl smiles, "Always be a Good Customer, okay?"

Going Dutch

Going Dutch

©1997 Jen Sorensen

WHEN I WAS YOUNGER, I DREAMED OF MOVING TO NEW YORK AND BECOMING AN ILLUSTRIOUS PAINTER OF THE ABSURD.

I THINK WE SORELY UNDERESTIMATE THE AESTHETIC POTENTIAL OF ANIMALS IN SPACE...

"Blast Off Giraffe-Style"

DUE TO A COMPLEX SERIES OF EVENTS, HOWEVER, I NOW FIND MYSELF AS AN ILLUSTRIOUS GROCERY STORE CASHIER IN THE HEART OF PENNSYLVANIA DUTCH COUNTRY.

URF!

LAVENDER HAIR →

Glamour Kitty

BINK!

MY BOSS SERIOUSLY **IS** NED FLANDERS FROM "THE SIMPSONS."

HI DIDDLY HO, JEN! YOU CAN GO ON BREAK NOW! ENJOY!

IN A STRANGE WAY, THOUGH, I KIND OF LIKE IT. THE PLACE IS SO DOG-GONED **EARNEST**— NOT A TRACE OF PRETENSE ANYWHERE! THE BAG BOYS TALK ABOUT **CARS!**

DUDE, I HAD'ER UP TO 110 THE OTHER NIGHT ON ROUTE 30!

NO WAY!

THERE'S SOMETHING REASSURINGLY **REAL** ABOUT SELLING PECULIAR CUTS OF MEAT TO OLD-TIMERS.

WOULD YOU LIKE YOUR PIG STOMACH IN A BAG, SIR?

I'LL WARN YOU RIGHT NOW ABOUT SCRAPPLE. SCRAPPLE IS CONSIDERED A PENNSYLVANIA DUTCH DELICACY. IT COMES IN GREYISH BRICKS AND CONSISTS MAINLY OF PIG SCRAPS.* DO NOT BE TEMPTED BY ITS CUTE NAME, UNLESS YOU CONSIDER YOURSELF VERY BRAVE!

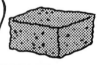

THE OTHER CASHIERS ARE FRIENDLY ENOUGH, EXCEPT FOR RUTH. RUTH IS TERMINALLY DISSATISFIED WITH THE WAY **EVERYTHING** IS DONE, AND VERY LOUDLY ANNOUNCES THINGS WE'D RATHER NOT KNOW ABOUT.

YEAH, MAH BOWELS WERE ACTIN' UP AGAIN THIS MORNING!

THEN THERE'S ETHEL. SHE WAS A DANCER AND COCKTAIL WAITRESS IN NEW YORK IN THE 1940s!

SO YOU DON'T KNOW WHAT TO DO WITH YOURSELF?

DON'T WORRY ABOUT IT! WHEN YOU'RE 22 YOU'RE YOUNG AND STUPID ANYWAY.

BINK! BINK!

ETHEL GIVES ME HOPE.

JUST LIVE HARD AND FAST, DEARIE! IT'S THE ONLY WAY!

* Including pig snouts.

JORDAN ROBINSON

Non Stop Go

5:46 P.M. "STILL HOT?" GRUNTS THE MAN at the door, bypassing any salutations. "Should be," I reply. He glares, "We've been waiting over an hour and a half." I know he's lying but so am I. "And we're *pissed off.*" I can see that. My degree in International Diplomacy hasn't proved totally worthless. It's taught me to always attempt to be affable. "Sorry, they gave me the wrong address." "Hmmph," his wife snorts, "I thought they were supposed to be good with numbers." The situation's beyond amelioration. Due to my co-worker's slap-happy packing job, the bottom of the grease-soaked bag of tepid Cantonese cuisine is going to give out any minute now. I want to be far away when that happens. I thrust the bag into his hands. "Thirty-five bucks." Mr. Surly hands me a twenty, a ten, and a five. He displays a loonie in his outstretched palm. "Get here pronto next time and it's yours." What an incentive. "You tell your boss he can shove a wok up his ass." Another oak door slams in my face.

6:10 P.M. "Why take so long?" Rik, my implacable boss, whines immediately upon my return. "Twenty-five kilometres in thirty minutes isn't long," I counter. "It borders on reckless." He shoots me a dubious look, "I am gonna have to keep my eyes on you." "And you gave me the wrong address for the first one —" "Just go pack the orders," he interrupts. "You go by the number." Bills are strewn over the counter. A deluge of delivery orders is nigh.

6:50 P.M. Time is money! Cough it up! The Rottweiler continues to lunge at me, defiling my jeans. The *hausfrau* returns to the door with her long lost purse. "Don't worry about Sika, she's harmless." I know that. But these Levi's cost me seventy. "What were the injuries again?" "Thirty-nine and five cents." "Gotta have that five cents," she snaps, ferreting out a coin. "Those Orientals," she mutters. "They're tigers, aren't they, always fighting for a buck." Yes, so unlike you and I.

7:01 P.M. The engine bleats and drones before dying. Start, you bastard! I turn the key a fourth time. We have ignition. Onward.

7:21 P.M. I trip over a rake and stumble toward the steps. Why do people make a point of killing their lights when they order food for delivery? I focus my anger on the bronze lion's head, bashing it into the door with excessive force. A jovial, adipose man answers, shouting in mock panic, "Quick, Linda, hide the dogs! He'll catch them and roast them." Laughter follows. Not from me. I've heard the line too many times. He starts peeling bills from his wallet. "Do you get the tip? I'm not funding any refugees."

"Those Orientals," she mutters. "They're tigers, aren't they, always fighting for a buck." Yes, so unlike you and I.

7:48 P.M. Scooping out rice that has the consistency of cement. Rik's embroiled in a heated argument on the phone. "That is just the way we cook it! Okay, okay. I am not gonna spend time with you." He hangs up. "Fuck. *Suck!* Those people say the Szechuan Chicken is not cooked. You gotta go back and refund it. Check the food and make sure. If they eat twenty percent or more you don't give them any money back." I nod in concurrence, but there's no way I'm going to fulfill my promise. Once I hit the road, I call the shots. "No, push with two hands," Rik advises as I struggle to close a bag with our antediluvian stapler. I try once more and fail. "It's jammed —" "You are a girl," Rik sneers and tries himself. "Fuck suck," he bitches. "Is jammed!"

8:20 P.M. Forced to double park in a bus zone outside a high-rise. With carte blanche commercial plates, I can park almost anywhere. As long as I'm able to exit forward. The oxidizing heap I'm driving no longer affords the luxury of reverse. I buzz 404. A woman appears in the lobby five minutes later, sporting shades and silicone enhancement. Redolent of beer. Clad in a tank-top, tie-dye scarves, tight jeans and purple boots, everything about her screams rock groupie. I position our portable credit machine. She fixes her fly and announces that she has to go, a taxi awaits. "The VISA's upstairs. Just knock. Whatever happens, the money's there." Intrigued, I take the elevator to the fourth floor and knock on the door. And wait. A familiar resinous odour is emanating from within. I hear movement. The door opens and an unshaven man stares at me, none too friendly. "Hi, Chinese food, I was told the VISA was here." "Uhhh," he grumbles and closes the door. Odd behaviour. I knock again, well aware that I can't return to the restaurant without endeavouring to get rid of the food. Knock-knock. The door opens, revealing the same man, who has donned a Bud Light cap during the interim. I try to put things plainly. "I was told downstairs the VISA was here." He answers plainly, "I didn't order any fucking food!" and slams the door. Onward.

8:46 P.M. "You get lost or something?" Rik jeers as I enter the kitchen. I ignore his *de rigueur* greeting and apprise him of the thirty dollars worth of rejected food. "Oh, *suck!* People can't just order and not accept it. Why didn't you tell them that?" "I did my best." He waves me away with disgust. "Just go pack the orders. You go by the number." Paper bags everywhere. The rush shows no sign of abating. "You, me, your girlfriend, Seymour Street tonight. I pay," the wok cook bellows at me with a grin, convivially slapping his back pocket to further demonstrate his willingness. I flatly refuse.

9:15 P.M. Hammering on the door in the pissing rain. To no avail. As I turn to leave, locks start clicking and sliding. "Hey, boy. Been waiting long?" "About five minutes." "Seriously? I don't know why we didn't hear you." This statement from a man who stands before me bathrobed and beaming while his flushed grinagog of a wife hovers behind him in a nightgown. The portrait of innocence. He rustles up some cash. "You wouldn't have any pot on you, would you?" he inquires. I tell him I wish I did. Not that I'd give him any. Just 'cause I'm over twenty and delivering Chinese food doesn't make me a dealer. I haven't hit that low yet.

9:25 P.M. Rik barks orders staccato, infuriated that our waitress has just walked out due to unwanted fondling from the wok cook. I commiserate with my co-worker about the dire shortage of refined customers. Rik watches us like a hawk. Socializing's verboten on his territory. "Fucking *gais,*" he sniggers. (*Gai* meaning chicken, as in a little piece of chicken; i.e., a hooker.) "You can't just keep talking. You gotta watch with your eyes or you fuck up all the orders." The wok cook says my cohort's mother has big breasts and that explains where he got his. "*Dao lai mogo chow hai,*" my cohort retorts, the latest expression we've learned from the headwaiter. Can't say this job has no cultural benefits.

9:42 P.M. Back at the high-rise. Apparently they'd like their meal now. "I'm so sorry," gushes the aging party girl I encountered earlier in the lobby. "Come on in." My entrance is met with the standard cry of, "Hey, you ain't no wee Chinee." Laughs. What wit. Someone's chortling, "He's on the bathroom floor in the fetal position." I place the bag on the counter. The food obviously hasn't been reheated. No doubt that's payback from Rik, who'd reheat it only if the delay was our fault. Several men in baseball caps are seated on black leather couches in the living room. None of them lack a beverage. The woman asks where the VISA is. That's what I wanna know. The man I had the misfortune of meeting earlier approaches, reeling and staggering, coke-faced. "I'm not footing all the fucking bills," he tells her in a guttural tone. "You pay your own damn way." She reaches for her purse while he stares at me menacingly. "Who the hell are you, anyway?" he snarls. "I'm really sorry," the woman repeats. "I'm just delivering the food," I explain. "Yeah, well, fuck you and the horse you rode in on!" More laughs. "Excuse me?" "Easy, buddy, easy," a tall man urges. He leads the violently incapacitated man away. The belligerent sinks to his knees and grips the air fiercely, then rises and wanders off into another room. I wonder whether he has access to any knives or other sharp objects. I spot a bag of golf clubs nearby. "No, wait, I have to give you a tip," the woman protests as I head for the door with the bills she hands me. The tall man goes to the counter and helps her scrape up some silver. "How much do you want?" "Whatever you think." "Oh, come on." She exhales, flaunting considerable cleavage, and intones, "How much do you want?" The tall man leers at her and winks at me, "She's a stripper, you know."

10:35 P.M. Finally sitting. Savouring Cashew Gai Ding and a mound of steamed rice doused with soy sauce. "What, you still eating?" ubiquitous Rik exclaims behind me. "You gotta eat fast, you got two more orders. Go by the number." No time to ruminate. I fear these nine-minute meals will soon induce dyspepsia.

11:00 P.M. "Thirty-three." The man in the Eagles t-shirt whistles, "I can remember when dinner for three was fifteen bucks." I can't. Anyhow, I don't set the price. I just deliver it. He starts raiding the drawers. "I say we forget the bill and he just stays and smokes a joint with us," suggests a shirtless man rolling a doobie on the coffee table. "Yeah, right," I scoff. Smoke one j with three thirty-something losers for a thirty-three-dollar order. It would have to be some exceptionally wicked hash. Fairly hammered, they don't take kindly to my refusal. "Oh, we're not cool enough, huh?" the bare-chested man spits. His friend snatches my wallet from my back pocket. "Hey, this guy's loaded." I snatch it back. "How 'bout some of this, eh?" he shouts and starts squeezing my buttock. I grab his arm and push him away. He backs off, spilling beer on the carpet. "Just kidding man, just kidding." "Hey, stay with us and we'll show you how to really party," the shirtless man offers, flicking a Zippo and igniting a fat joint. The other two are eyeing me. I don't like the atmosphere at all. "Hey, don't tip the guy much. I mean, we do something for him, he does something for us," the boisterous man babbles. You wish. I seize the wad of bills the Eagles fan extends and get the fuck out.

JOKE'S ON THEM. Back in the saddle, unscathed, I discover they've given me two fives too many, bringing my take to twelve bucks. My elation's evanescent. A minute later, the beater conks out on the main thoroughfare. I stare down at the dash, seeking an indication of what's wrong. All I see is the "FUCK YOU" that's remained finger scrawled in the thick dust for over a year. Cars bullet past, honking viciously. I could just step out and walk away.... But I don't. This job's no sinecure but there are worse places to be exploited at. And hey, the money's decent.

MICHELLE GAVIN

Hazardous Duty

SOMETIMES THE *whoosh* of oncoming projectiles made me more than a little nervous. I tried to be a professional, to keep my cool, but I couldn't always stave off the panic. The men around me were out of control – ignoring their own peril, they wielded their instruments wildly, driven by heat, alcohol, and lust. I considered asking if I could wear a helmet, but realized that it might give me heat stroke. Besides, it would have diminished my tips considerably. You see, I wasn't a photojournalist in Beirut or an undercover cop. I was driving the cabana cart at a golf course in the middle of summer in Phoenix, Arizona. I favored minimal clothing for both remunerative and survival purposes.

MY VEHICLE, a luxury stretch golf cart, was painted neon pink with a matching pink canopy trimmed in shiny yellow fringe. In the back I carried three coolers full of beer, rapidly melting ice, and some token soft drinks. My duties consisted of tearing around the golf course, stopping whenever I saw signs of life, and perkily shouting:

"Nice chip! Care for a beverage?"

"Ooohh, nasty slice. Console yourself with something cold?"

"Great putt. How 'bout another round?"

THINK of me as sort of a cocktail waitress on wheels. In hell.

CRUISING around a golf course populated by drunken, overheated men day after day had hazards beyond the sand-trap on 7. The golf balls themselves were the most obvious – nearly every day one would ricochet off the cart or threaten to tear through the canopy, re-opening my internal debate about the costs and benefits of a helmet. The other hazard was simply the clientele. Consider the kind of people who golf in mid-afternoon in a Phoenix summer. It's about 117° outside. Touching the metal shaft of a club that's been sitting in that kind of heat could conceivably brand a person for life. Now consider the kind of people who golf *and* drink heavily in mid-afternoon in a Phoenix summer. Some safety precautions were in order.

WHEN they looked sufficiently heat-dazed and harmless, I'd get out of the cart and dash across the green to hand over the Budweiser and make the change. If they looked like trouble (asking why I wasn't driving around in a bikini like the cabana girl at a competing course), I'd sort of toss the beers at them, maintaining one foot on the cart's accelerator, ready to floor it down the fairway should things get ugly. With such men – *"Why don't you come over here and check out my biggest club, baby"* – I'd get out of the cart only in the case of a medical emergency. These were irritatingly frequent – that sun and alcohol combination made for a near-epidemic of heat-stroke. (Although, to be fair, heavy drinking in such temperatures did seem to encourage big tips. Dizziness and headaches made the simplicity of "keep the change" an irresistible option for the distressed golfer.) I'd haul the casualties back to the clubhouse, making wrenching decisions about whether to rush them directly to air-conditioned safety or to take a slower route, pausing to do business with the generous foursome on 16. Modify the earlier image – now I'm not just a cocktail waitress, but also a *de facto* paramedic . . . in very short shorts.

Think of me as sort of a cocktail waitress on wheels. In hell.

I CAME away from that summer with a boosted bank account, an enduring hatred of golf, possibly skin cancer, definitely premature wrinkling. Back at my eastern college, I glorified the cabana position on a job application in order to move up a rung on the ladder of humbling employment and out of the warzone. By assuring the manager that I had waitressing experience, I landed a job that required me to take serious evasive action when surrounded by lascivious kitchen staff, but did not involve projectiles of any kind.

HE

LP

JO ANNE C. HEEN

Jo Anne Doesn't Want to Work Here Anymore

"THIS IS JO ANNE in Customer Service. How may I help you?"

"I want my money and I want it now!" the New Yorker bawled into the phone. "My son is a lawyer, he'll sue you!" While she screamed and threatened, I sat back in my chair and mimed slitting my wrists. Five minutes later she ran out of steam and I took the opportunity to say, "I'd be happy to credit your account for twenty-four cents, Ma'am." Mollified, the customer thanked me and hung up.

I'm a phone operator in the catalogue sales and customer service departments for one of the biggest outdoor clothing outfitters in the Pacific Northwest. There are only two things I hate about my job: the customers, and everything else. I knew it was going to suck from the get-go, but I was new in town and needed to make the rent. Looking for the job from hell? Here it is.

My eight-hour workday is filled with upset, angry, and petty people who cling to the misconception that I personally and deliberately ruined their day. Order a suitcase and receive a lamp instead? My fault. Was that green sweater monogrammed with green thread? I was on the sewing machine that day. Wait until the day before your mother's birthday to order her gift from the clearance catalogue? I just bought the last one, but only because I knew you were going to need it. Sorry,

sorry, sorry, please don't cry, it's not your fault you mailed a package back to us but put the wrong address on it. I'll be more than happy to deal with the crazies at the post office for you.

It's not true that I'm a first-class bitch, despite how I sound. I really want to provide great customer service and make the customer happy. Sometimes the customer makes that impossible. Yell at me because an item is sold out. Call me names because we don't carry size 60 jeans. Take ten minutes telling me why you won't give me your credit card number even though that's the only way I can place the order. Call from Japan and insist on placing an order while knowing only four words in English.

Management doesn't help ease the tension any. The operators are constantly getting called into the office for scolding. The current Big Sin is long call times. Call time is how long it takes the operator to take an order. I can't help it if a customer has to go up to the third floor of her house to search for her credit card. That takes time. I can't stop a customer from asking me about the weather. I once got yelled at because I took three seconds to make an unnecessary comment to a customer. The ten minutes it took to tell me about it didn't matter, though. My boss has a special way to keep me in line: she threatens to fire me. Well, *she* wouldn't fire me, she's quick to assure me, but *they* would, if my many infractions were to be discovered. However, a good operator is rewarded with a gold star. Yep, just like in kindergarten.

I hate surprises, but that's what I get each week when I pick up my schedule. Start times and days off are never the same. One week, I might start at six A.M. Saturday, Sunday, and Monday, get Tuesday off, Wednesday, come in at seven A.M. Thursday off. Friday, I've got the six-thirty shift. The next week, I'll work the seven-thirty to four P.M. shift, with Saturday and Monday off. If I'm lucky, I'll get two days off in a row. I'm rarely lucky. Try scheduling a dentist appointment. Try planning Sunday brunch.

Oh, the job isn't all bad. Payday is great. The day I quit will be fantastic.

Happiness is
Pat Pedersen-Serving-You-At-Sears

OKAY. START WITH THE application. Start the lying here. My honest (maybe a tiny bit hostile) approach isn't working. Personnel managers, bosses, supervisors, they all ask the wrong questions. Like, why do I want to come work at their company. So I go, well, I quit law school, I had to give back the financial aid, I'm *sooo* broke, and they go all quiet. Like I'd want to work there for some other reason besides money. When they ask at the end of the interview, do you have any questions, that's the question I'd like to ask: Why the hell would I want to work here? Put it back on them. The way it is now, there's a point in every interview when they start breathing real loud through their noses. This is when I tell them that about half their interview questions are illegal. Just a humanitarian effort on my part to update them on civil rights legislation and bring them into the last half of the goddamn century. And they get offended.

But I've wised up. I'm going to lie and if that doesn't work, I've got a back-up plan. If I don't get a job by January 1, I'm driving my mortgaged Toyota off Dash Point Road and into Puget Sound. That's six weeks away. But I'm no Johnny-Jump-The-Gun. I'm willing to participate in some serious debasement before I buy that last tank of gas. And that's what I'm doing now, applying at Sears. Temporary Christmas help.

I'm not writing on the application, under qualifications, *None*. I do not plan to state in the interview that I won't shut up about the evils of capitalism. I won't shout my credo: You could be screwing instead of shopping! I'll keep my mouth shut during Orientation and Training. I'm willing to toe the line. Last week, I was unhired by the Bon Marché during Orientation and Training. It wasn't my fault, but hey, is it ever? It was a bad beginning. Fourteen would-be sales clerks, jittery eyes, and our similes waddled up like used Kleenex. A woman (I guess it was a woman, all Revloned and Rubensteined, can you do more than guess?) presents the day's agenda: We'll learn the Register. They always take this shit so seriously, like we have to prepare to ascend to the heights of Mount fucking Everest, become one with The Register or The Whatever, as if it's almost as important as nuclear weapons or STDs. But first, we're going to hear from security.

The goons slouch in. Scruffed up. The-Woman-In-Charge titters: "Bet a shoplifter would never catch on to them!" A few would-bes tee-hee. My hackles are way up. Bad sign. Goon number one narrows his eyes. He's gonna give us rookies the low down:

You gotta watch out all the time, 'cause they're everywhere. First off, stolen cards. Here's how to retrieve a bad card. Stick it *inside* the register while you run a check. You wanna do this 'cause you get ten bucks for it. Now, here's what to look out for: Black guy with a card, Asian woman with a card, any woman without a wedding ring got a card. Snatch that card. Put it in the register. Ten bucks for you. Thieves, lifters, we hav'ta get 'em. Maybe you see somebody. Looks like they want something real bad. *Don't do anything!* Call us. Hide. Go in the dressing room. Get behind a rack of clothes. Anywhere they can't see you. Give 'em a chance to rip something off. Leave it to us. We'll get 'em.

My grandmother, when something surprised her, used to say, "I swear." So do I. But I really swear. Sometimes my mouth is a toilet I just can't flush. It fills up and runs out. I cuss and curse them 'til my mouth is almost dry and then I turn to The-Woman-In-Charge. I switch tones and clarify the technical and legal terms of entrapment. I threaten to take their racist, sexist, illegal *et* damn *cetera* to the media. I'm out of the Bon before the ink blots on my W-4. I stuff my self-righteous self into the Toyota and drive off in a huff. Now I'm really broke. I'd bought panty-hose to wear as part of my ordinary person disguise. I don't think I can return 'em.

So. Here we go. Orientation and Training at Sears. Here The-Woman-In-Charge wears little snowman earrings and addresses us in a cheerfully psychotic voice: *We know you all love to shop or you wouldn't be here! We want this to be fun! We're giving each of you ten dollars to go out and shop at Sears! Oh, there's a catch.*

She titters. I'm starting to wonder, is tittering a job requirement? She goes on: *You have to give back to Sears whatever you buy! You can't even keep the change! Be sure to save the receipt! See, we work day and night to improve customer service. We have to know how our clerks are doing. You're the judge. When you get back, fill out this form.*

SHE WAVES THE FORM like it's a flag from an important country. *Now you've got fifteen minutes! Remember, you're undercover. Don't let the salesclerk catch on. And have some fun!*

I'm on my soapbox before the door shuts. I'm Spencer Tracy, Norma Rae, Emma Goldman. "C'mon. They're giving us minimum wage to spy on workers just like us. Next week they'll be asking some poor sucker in clerk training to spy on you. Here's what we've gotta do: Get out here, spend the money, get back here and fill out the best report possible."

They file out like obedient soldiers. I have a creepy feeling that my fellow workers are so discouraged they'd follow the instructions of whoever talked last. But, I figure, enlisted or voluntary, we're all in this together. I spend my ten on Scrabble, guessing the clerks in Toys are the most hassled. I review the reports before The-Woman-In-Charge returns. All the checks are in the good-to-excellent columns. No one rats me out. We learn The Register. We're told: Report tomorrow.

Sunday. All my comrades get assignments but me. I'm trying to figure out if hijacking the training process is an arrestable offense when the woman, you know who I mean, says, "Patricia, we didn't want the others to feel bad. But because you're a college graduate, we think you can handle floating." It's a privilege. I'm to go wherever I'm needed. First stop, Yard Goods.

I am not going to fit in. For me, all things domestic possess the dual qualities of terror and boredom. I was kicked out of junior high for threatening to sew the teacher's mouth shut, and the same kind of malice comes over me whenever I'm surrounded by "women's work." I figure my best strategy is to hide out 'til my next assignment. I skulk around bolts of dark taffeta, scratchy plaids, fluorescent polyester. Hiding is always harder than working, especially if you're wearing a badge which proclaims, "Happiness-Is-Pat-Pedersen-Serving-You-At-Sears," an accessory I plan to wear into the afterlife, providing it's not seized as contraband at the Pearly Gates. I dodge customers and appear at The Register just as the Supreme Being, the floating supervisor, comes into view. "Regular girl's sick," she spouts. "You're needed in Candy and Nuts."

Needed in Candy and Nuts! I move so fast the bottom of my feet burn. Hot cashews going round and round on three tiers of a lazy susan. Huge chunks of fudge: dark chocolate and rocky road. Soft candies, hard candies, sugared orange slices, Gummy Bears. I have a sweet tooth the size of a shopping bag. I have no money. I'm in heaven.

The catch is off to one side. A scale the size of a small jet. The needle on the scale is so thin it's almost invisible. I didn't even know you could divide smaller than ounces. Next to the scale is a chart listing all the candies and nuts and cryptic directions for converting those measurements into an actual retail price. I'm getting shooting pains in my eyes just looking at it. I look away. Multiplying, dividing, yeah. Fractions? Way back, I had a pair of tonsils turning my throat into a pain highway. Through coincidence, and no fault of my own, those tonsils were ripped from my throat at the very moment every other third grader was learning, "Now you reverse, now you don't" calculations. I confess, I never caught up. But a gal's got to move on. I stuff my mouth full of candy and go to work.

Christmas season. People are shopping. Shopping makes people very hungry. I keep busy. I keep a mouthful of cashews, chocolate, one of whatever anybody else is having. I charge whatever seems fair. Maybe a little less. I really don't believe Sears would want me to risk going high. Cheat the public? What kind of Happiness-Is-Pat-Pedersen-Serving-You-At-Sears would that be? People keep coming back for more. They love me. I smile through my M&M-stained teeth. The M&Ms are spectacular. No packaging to get in the way of the flavour. Their little shells crack open. A wave of chocolate breaks over my tongue. A little salty from the peanuts. I like that. I'm dreaming, fantasizing a future at Sears. Finally, a place for me! Two men in dark suits march up to the counter. I know in a flash these guys are not here for the candy. Bad at math, but I'm psychic.

The tall one talks through a mouth that's sucked too many sourballs. "We've been watching you, miss. Just what do you think you're doing?"

"You've been watching me! Just what the hell do you think you're doing!" I've watched enough presidential press conferences to know what to do when you're guilty. I'm talking full volume with a mouth full of hot nuts. Little flecks of cashews are threatening the front of their suits. "You saw the scale was broken! Why didn't you send for help? I'm trying to keep the customers happy here, and I could use a little back-up. Who the hell do you work for, Sears or J.C. Penney?" I spit and swear my way out the don't-look-back double doors. I've got a stomach I can barely squeeze behind the wheel, a plastic badge, four more weeks.

Baby Seals Have It Easy

I SPENT JUST OVER A YEAR as a door-to-door fundraiser for a certain environmental group in Vancouver. A year doesn't sound like much, but in this case it makes me a grizzled veteran. Door canvassers are the trench-footed, shell-shocked, expendable cannon fodder of the environmental movement. Most burn out after a week or two; a handful last a month; and only the most resilient, dedicated, and/or desperate stick it out longer.

Here's how it works. You show up in the afternoon for "briefing," where you dodge cockroaches (pesticides are frowned upon) while the canvass director brings you up to speed on the latest developments on the eco front. Any one of said developments is enough to turn your hair white. Half the Malaysian rainforest on fire. Brain cancer a leading cause of death in a certain pulp-mill town. A press release, signed by over half the living Nobel Prize recipients, declaring that the human race had about twenty years to live. After a week of this, you start looking for ways to mainline Prozac.

Then you pile into a decrepit van with squishy brakes and frayed seat belts and head out to your "turf" – usually some godforsaken dogpatch of a suburb – to knock on doors, explain issues, and ask for donations until about nine o'clock in the evening. If you're lucky, it's not raining. (As this was Vancouver, I was seldom lucky.)

You'd think most people would be sympathetic. Guess again. The corporations that are wrecking the planet have huge public-relations budgets whose whole *raison d'etre* is to smear people like us. As a result, lots of people think environmentalists are the bad guys. I've been called an anarchist, a terrorist, a communist, a fascist, and a Tool of Satan. Half the people I meet think we're all getting rich off "eco-hysteria." The other half think we're on welfare. (One guy somehow accused me of both.) I've been screamed at by housewives, bitten by chihuahuas, sprayed with bleach by teenagers, punched by loggers, and chased down dirt roads by mouth-breathing pinheads in muscle cars.

In Vernon, B.C., I opened up the newspaper to find my name and description in the Crime Stoppers column, and a $1000 reward out for my arrest. It turned out that one of my "doors" from the week before hated our group so much that he fingered me as a fraud artist. (Crime Stoppers didn't even bother to contact our office to find out if I was for real.) I spent the next two working days – on $800 a month, you can't afford to take a day off – dodging police and amateur bounty hunters until my field manager could arrange a ride out of town.

Obviously, the pay sucks. And the working hours – you usually get home around eleven o'clock – tend to preclude a normal social life. You soon find yourself trapped in this incestuous little scene, drinking, gossiping, sharing apartments, and sleeping with other canvassers. It's sort of like joining a cult, but without the consolation of, say, knowing the space aliens are coming to pick you up.

Most canvassers crack from sheer frustration and despair. Either they quit, or they stay on and sink into depression, alcoholism, and/or raging, venom-soaked bitterness. On a canvassing trip to the Yukon, I watched a field manager go berserk, screaming at us for two hours before storming off into the howling wilderness. Nine months later I went off more or less the same way. The only surprise is that it took that long.

SIMA RABINOWITZ

How I Got Fired From the Ladies' Hosiery Division of One of the Finest Department Stores in the Midwest

ONE   "Can I try these on?" A young woman in imitation designer career-wear (the shiny, limp navy lining of her narrow skirt dipping below the hemline) held out a package of Hanes Silk Reflections (Barely Beige). She had already slipped the hose off the flat cardboard insert inside the cellophane wrapping, stretching her hand dangerously wide inside the exposed waistband.

"No," I said, taking the package from her, though I knew she hadn't extended it in my direction for that purpose. I began to fold the fabric over the now slightly-crumpled cardboard.

"These damn things cost $5.25 a pair and they'll probably get a run in them the first time I wear them. I don't understand why I can't at least see how they fit." She reached out and reclaimed the package.

I wanted to take her side. I really did. I wanted to tell her that this was precisely the point, that Hanes was counting on her and on thousands of women like her to run their nylons by noon, that she was lucky if she got through the day without a snag or a hole or a tear somewhere precisely the length of her index finger. I wanted to suggest that she wear slacks to work, sensible shoes, cotton socks. I wanted to say, "Sure, go ahead, at this price you might as well find out how they feel."

But I knew what was expected of me, and I took my job seriously. It seemed that it was my duty to defend not only the merchandise itself, but the very foundation (pun intended) of the industry.

"Well," I said earnestly, "let me try to explain this to you. In the supermarket when you want to try a brand of cookies you've never bought before, for the sake of argument let's say Fig Newtons, can you take the box off the shelf, open it up, bite into a Fig Newton and then put the box back on the shelf if you decide you don't want it after all?"

"Do you have something very, very sheer that is also very, very durable?"

Silence. She stood perfectly still for what seemed like an eternity, but was probably only ten seconds or so. Then she drew her arm back behind her head and hurled the package over the counter at me as if it were a flat, square frisbee. Or perhaps a box of Fig Newtons. Since she had already turned to leave before she took aim, the Silk Reflections never made it over the counter. Instead, they landed in the next aisle where a customer, concentrating intently on making her selection, frowned and stepped lightly over them as she approached the Jockey fall collection, a forest theme – mint, olive, cypress, sage – all handsome shades of green.

TWO It was probably a mistake to have developed an elaborate set of responses to two of the most frequently asked questions in Ladies' Hosiery: 1. "Do you have something very, very sheer that is also very, very durable?" and 2. "Am I supposed to wear panties under my pantyhose?"

THREE I was never very good at math. All the same, it did occur to me that six percent of $250 (the average price of a coat, fourth floor,

Women's Outer Wear) was considerably more than six percent of $5 (the average price of a pair of pantyhose, first floor, Ladies' Hosiery). To be truthful, our commission was not actually six percent of everything we sold. It was six percent of everything we sold above and beyond our required hourly minimum quota, which in Ladies' Hosiery was $75 an hour.

That figure (pun intended) translates into something on the order of twenty-five pairs of store-brand thigh-highs sans reinforced toes, or twenty pairs of Evan Picone sheer-to-the-waist off-black pantyhose, or fifteen twin-packs of "Round-the-Clock" all-day-support knee-hi's, or ten pairs of Givenchy "Body Gleamers" in Sparkling Champagne, or five pairs of Donna Karan's silky "Opaque Satins" with control tops. Or some combination thereof.

My mother, who is decidedly better at math than me, suggested I simply saunter upstairs and sell a couch or two (fifth floor, Household Furnishings). I knew that items requiring home delivery were probably out of the question. But, even though we were discouraged from leaving our departments to make sales in other divisions, I was dearly hoping to sell something with a triple digit price tag.

Late one weekday evening, when the store was quiet except for the muffled sounds of boredom and the clerk from Belts & Scarves (first floor, around the corner from Ladies' Hosiery) cashing out early, I spent close to half an hour helping our only customer pick out a pair of nylons to match her wedding dress. Deliberations concluded, we walked to the register and, dutifully, I asked what else she might need – tights to complement her outfit for the reception, or a pair of lacy socks to spruce up her jeans for the rehearsal dinner. I was certain she'd say "No, thanks" since it had taken her a very long time to decide on the crystal whites, and she had balked at the prices and selected the least expensive pair. So I was already ringing up the sale and bagging her purchase when instead she said, "I need a dress. I'm going to France for my honeymoon, and I want a chic, stylish, April-in-Paris kind of dress." (Third floor, Women's

Designer Originals, I thought, and off we went.)

That quarter I received the largest commission cheque ever earned by an employee in Ladies' Hosiery. And I almost didn't find it, my narrow company mailbox was so crowded with notices, all in boldface type, announcing sternly: EMPLOYEE'S (sic) WILL NO LONGER RECEIVE COMMISSION DOLLARS FOR ITEMS NOT ORIGINATING IN THE DEPARTMENT TO WHICH THEY ARE ASSIGNED.

FOUR In the universe of Ladies' Hosiery, the biggest night of the year is New Year's Eve. On what turned out to be my last such occasion, it was, as always, a mad dash and scramble for just the right shade and shape, the perfect glimmer and shimmer, the tightest fit and the sleekest look.

Customers swarmed the narrow areas around the designer displays and specialty items. Behind the registers, we rang up package after package of sheer black hose. Surrounded by noisy, eager shoppers clamoring for attention and our expert advice, we worked at a furious pace.

All at once, we heard a terrible, awful wailing from the depths of the Christian Dior racks. Concerned, I rushed breathlessly toward the sound of this piercing cry until I located a thin, elegantly dressed woman who was quite nearly hysterical.

"Aren't there any more of these in size B?" she moaned, gesturing wildly.

"Sold out," I informed her, "but there are dozens of others, nearly identical." And I offered to help her find something equally suitable.

"Oh, no. I simply must have these," she insisted. She began to wail again. Louder this time.

I tried, in vain, to explain that much of what we did have in stock was made by the very same mill that had produced the type she was so attached to, that I could offer her a dozen pairs similar in shape, shade, texture. But she wouldn't be swayed from either her brand loyalty or her agony.

"Oh, God. What am I going to do? What am I going to do?"

Suddenly she stopped short, composed herself, straightened her shoulders. She turned to glare at me, then stepped forward, her face close, too close to mine, her breath hot and sharp. "And now what, young lady?" she said. Sometimes I wonder if I only imagined her hand on her hip.

"Hmmm," I waited for a long, slow second. "Hmmm," I said thoughtfully, pausing briefly, deliberately between each word. "I guess this will be the end of the world as we know it."

But, as it happened, it was only the end of my short-lived career in Ladies' Hosiery.

A Load of Fun at the Toy Store

"AND AFTER I GOT OUT OF PRISON, I told everybody in Sudbury to call me Willy, cuz that's my new name."

I sort of smiled and casually asked Willy what he had done to go to prison.

He belched in reply, blowing his Coke-flavoured breath in my face, and said: "For stabbing a homosexual in a bar after he tried to pick me up." My smile faltered slightly and I turned around to pick up another box.

It was a cold and lonely December night and I couldn't help but wonder why what should have been a dream job, working a barely supervised night shift at the world's biggest toy store, sucked as much as it did.

The midnight to morning shift can be an evil experience, even for those of us who enjoy late nights. Sure, you get used to it after a while, but I didn't stick around long enough to do that.

It was at one of those times when I would have taken almost any job offered me, a situation that happens more often than not. I spotted the ad in the paper, applied, and assumed I wouldn't get the job.

When they called me back two weeks later to say I was hired, I was quite surprised. Jobs are sometimes hard to come by for the unskilled among us. As it turned out, this one required little in both the skills and brains departments. It was the Christmas season and the store's only concern was keeping the shelves stocked for rosy-faced consumers.

Not surprisingly, my first night was shit as I struggled to remain not only awake but active. I missed the next shift as a result while I considered whether or not the job was worth the pain. I think the management expected this sort of behaviour from new night shift employees because they didn't even call me.

When I showed up the next night a few minutes before midnight, they politely told me to call the next time I wasn't able to make it to work. I apologized profusely, making up a lame excuse about sleeping through the alarm clock. This seemed to placate them and my job was safe for the time being.

It was the kind of propaganda that the Nazis would have been proud of.

It wasn't long before I realized the job was going to be quite easy. My supervisor was only a year older than I was and not of the I'm-your-superior-therefore-you-are-below-me school of thought. She was an ex-new waver in her early twenties and not shy about her past, speaking freely of her teenage days of doing acid and going to all-night clubs in Toronto. The company's corporate ideology had yet to take a firm grasp on her.

There were eight of us on the night crew. Besides myself and Sudbury's infamous son Willy, there was Kevin, whom I once had the pleasure of working with at a bad fast food restaurant that went out of business about six months after it opened. He was a high school dropout whose favourite band was Guns 'n' Roses. He and his mother had recently become born again and they had taken in Willy, whose prison time made him "see the light," as a boarder.

Dan was another of my co-workers. He was a big fan of Andrew Dice Clay and would quote extensively from his repertoire whenever he got the chance.

After a few days we were called into the meeting room to watch some instructional videotapes.

Dan dug out "How to Deal with Internal Theft," and slid it into the machine. It was the kind of propaganda that the Nazis would have

been proud of. Video employees swathed in a puke-like mix of polyester colours proudly telling viewers about how they turned in their
fellow employees for stealing toys. "When they steal from the company, I feel like they're stealing from me," they droned. Stats and pie
charts flashed across the screen claiming that employee theft accounted
for millions of dollars in lost revenue each and every year. (This was
coming from a huge corporation that refused to give discounts to its
own employees, so it's no surprise that people would steal as a way of
getting something back.)

The next tape dealt with shoplifting and featured a wide spectrum
of thieves who pilfered toys on any given day. Rather than filmed
action, this video was made up of stills accented by an ominous voice-
over which gave chilling descriptions of the amoral thugs: *"The impulse
shoplifter enters the store with the intention of purchasing something, but
inexplicably winds up stealing. . . ."* The shot was of a middle-aged
woman shoving something into her purse while cautiously looking
over her shoulder to avoid detection.

Another memorable one was "Drug Addict." *"He comes in near closing
time and steals openly,"* intoned the video voice. The screen showed a pic-
ture of a glassy-eyed dirtbag leaning against the shelf trying to conceal a
large item under his too small jean jacket. Each segment was followed by
guffaws of laughter from everyone in the room. We obviously knew how
to make good use of company time.

No matter how bad it got at least we didn't have it as bad as the day-
time employees who were under constant supervision and forced to
wear those puke-coloured smocks. And, of course, we got to listen to
our own music.

When my tapes weren't on, however, it was pure torture. In addition
to Dan's lovely collection of metal, I had to deal with Willy's punk music.
Not surprisingly his idea of punk was somewhat different from mine.

"Yeah, I used to be a punk. Back in Sudbury," he said in a serious
tone. Willy wore off-the-rack TV lens glasses, sported a beard, and parted

his hair in the middle. To put it mildly, he looked like a redneck hick.

"I used to listen to all those punk bands," he continued, "the Cure, Siouxsie and the Banshees, Depeche Mode. I used to have a mohawk, too." He pulled his wallet out of his back pocket and dug out the only photo ID he had, a Money Mart cheque-cashing card. As I looked at his photo, I had to hold in the laugh that welled up inside me. TV lens glasses, a beard and, surprisingly enough, a mohawk.

When it was Willy's turn to put on a tape, he scurried up to the front and soon the synthetic strains of Depeche Mode were being piped out through the store's speakers. This would bring Willy into his own little world as he happily unloaded a box of Teenage Mutant Ninja Turtles while singing along to a song with lyrics about "little boys." The irony of the situation was beyond Willy's grasp but it brought a smile to my tired face.

I only stayed at the toy store for just over a month before I managed to find a better job. I didn't even give them notice. I just failed to show up for work one night. When the manager called to find out why I was late, I sort of chuckled and said: "Well, I won't be coming in tonight." When he asked me why, I replied: "Because I quit."

Last Call

I PRESSED A BLINKING LIGHT and answered one of our seven phone lines. "Senior Information," I said. There was no way to know what was coming. There never was.

Things were complicated from the start. Dora, a frantic elderly woman in Seattle, had called a friend of hers in California. The friend, who was worried about her, had called another friend who, in turn, was calling me. According to this third-hand source, Dora believed someone was going to "put her away."

Unlikely, I told the long distance caller. I explained the complex requirements for an involuntary commitment in Washington. Is Dora a danger to herself or others?

"I don't think so," the woman speculated.

"I'll look into it," I said.

I started by phoning Dora. She answered after several rings. Her voice was frail, her breathing laboured. "Just . . . a minute," she said. I heard jostling. Then her wheezing became temporarily muffled. This was the first of her frequent pauses for oxygen as she told me about the man who had come to her house earlier that morning and said "they" would come back to take her away.

"Who?" I asked.

"I don't know," she said.

"Did he say where 'they' would take you?"

"Please don't let them. I don't want to go back to the hospital," she pleaded.

Dora gave me permission to make some phone calls on her behalf, but I wasn't sure what to expect. Her account of a mysterious, threatening man didn't add up. Was her fear the product of a paranoid delusion (like that of another client, who believed a neighbour was stealing huge chunks out of the foundation of her house every night, or the one who swore someone was beaming the song "There's No Tomorrow" directly into her brain)?

As a long shot, I first contacted the government office responsible for involuntary commitments. I got stonewalled by confidentiality laws. When I hit dead ends with two other agencies, I decided to track down a social worker at the hospital Dora had mentioned. I found out Dora had discharged herself, against medical advice, the previous day. Her emphysema was critical. She would die soon if she didn't get back to the hospital. The social worker, believing that Dora was mentally incompetent to refuse medical treatment, had called the county mental health professionals, one of whom had indeed visited Dora that morning. He had agreed with the social worker. An involuntary commitment was imminent.

I braced myself and called Dora. I waited for her to wheel her oxygen tank to the phone and pick up. "People are worried about you," I said. I explained that she was putting her life in danger by not being at the hospital. I told her who the man was who had come to her house, what would happen next, why. Everything the mental health professional must have conveyed to her already, just hours before.

I couldn't tell how much Dora understood except that I was confirming her worst nightmare. Her voice elevated between sharp breaths.

"Can they really...make me...go back?...Can they?"

I wanted to lie. To tell her that it was all a mistake, no one would come. But I told the truth. As gently as I knew how, as gently as you can tell someone her life is to be prolonged against her will by order of a court. I was still talking when I heard the thud.

"Dora? Are you okay? Can you tell me what happened?"

Silence. I asked a colleague to dial 911 on another line. Three minutes later I heard loud knocking. Then, paramedics' voices. Finally, a click in my ear and the hum of a disconnection.

I waited. An hour and a half. Through a lunch I could barely swallow and an attempt at paperwork. Plenty long enough for the paramedics to get Dora to the hospital.

Before calling the social worker to confirm that Dora had been admitted, I re-dialed Dora's number. I'm not sure why. There was no point; her house would be empty. But a man's voice surprised me after the second ring. A police officer. They were just finishing up, he said. Dora was ready to be transported.

To the morgue.

Author Biographies

GRANT BUDAY · After working in a sawmill, door factory, hospital, then eight years in a mass production bakery inhaling several tons of flour dust, Grant Buday delivered advertising flyers. Then he taught English and discovered what an organ grinder's monkey must feel like, so he quit.

MARY CASEY lives and writes in Seattle, Washington. She's had many bad jobs, but *Feeding the Dreadfuls* is her first published story.

THE CHERNOBYL KID may be found muttering to himself and glowering menacingly at passers-by in Vancouver, where he lives, more or less.

EVE CORBEL is author and illustrator of *Power Parenting Your Teenager* and *The Little Greenish-Brown Book of Slugs*. Her comics and cartoons have also appeared in *Geist, Herizons, Ability Network, B.C. Bee Scene,* and other publications.

LARRY CRIST lives in Seattle, where he divides his time between acting and writing. Originally from California, he has lived many places and held many jobs to support himself in those places. He is working on a novel as well as a screenplay – anything to save him from more bad jobs.

ROB FERRAZ · After two years of telemarketing that helped pay for his BA in Journalism and Political Science from Concordia University, Rob is eager to get a "real" job. He publishes a 'zine called *Fist City* which, among other things, covers the topic of jobs he and many others have suffered through.

ALLEN FROST · Ever since eleventh grade, placing third in a contest nation-wide, Allan has been writing hundreds of stories and poems and up until now, seventeen book manuscripts. He lives with his wife and daughter in Ohio where he works in the library, saving his dollars until they can get back to the Pacific again.

MICHELLE GAVIN grew up in Phoenix, where she got her first job in her early teens taking inventory in the cavernous walk-in freezer of an ice-cream shop. She graduated from Georgetown University in 1996 with a degree in foreign service and a wealth of night-job experience serving food, filing folders, phoning alumni, and weeding gardens in the Washington, D.C. area. She is now studying International Relations at Oxford University on a Rhodes Scholarship. Due to work-permit technicalities and generous stipend checks, she is currently unemployed.

CAMILLA GIBB is currently writing, researching, thinking and breathing in Toronto. She is working on her first novel and has just been awarded a post-doctoral grant to conduct research with a small community of Ethiopian Muslims in Toronto.

ANDY HEALEY · Although he has worked as a bicycle messenger for the last eight years, Andy Healey is a dishwasher by trade. Andy enjoys the company of his dog and referring to himself in the third person. I should know as I am he.

JO ANNE C. HEEN is sorry she missed the age of courtesans. She would have made a good one. Jo Anne thinks these kinds of thoughts in Everett, Washington, where she lives with a projectile-vomiting cat.

SONJA L. INGEBRITSEN lives in Seattle. She received a Certificate in Advanced Literary Fiction from the University of Washington, and is currently working on a novel. "Last Call" is her first published story.

SHAUN LEVIN is a South African writer who lived in Israel for many years. His work has appeared in anthologies and magazines in Canada, England, Israel and the USA. He has been a soldier and a sandwich-maker. He now teaches creative writing and English as a second language.

JEANETTE LYNES · Originally from rural southern Ontario, Jeanette Lynes has lived and worked in many of Canada's provinces as well as Missouri and Seattle. Her poems have appeared in numerous journals and magazines. Most recently, her writing appeared in *Canadian Dimension, Zygote,* and *Atlantis: A Women's Studies Journal.* She has poetry forthcoming in *Firm Noncommittal.*

TIM MOERMAN swore he would never canvass door-to-door again. Apparently he lied. If he ever shows up on your doorstep, please write him a cheque.

BRUNO NADALIN, a seasoned verteran of many bad jobs, lives in Jersey City, NJ. His cartoons have appeared in a wide variety of independent publications, as well as in his own comic book, *Churn.* "Metropolitan Museum Security Guard" first appeared in the zine *McJob.*

HAL NIEDZVIECKI is author of *Smell It,* a book of short fiction published by Coach House Books and available on line at www.chbooks.com. He is editor of *Concrete Forest: The New Fiction of Urban Canada* (McClelland & Stewart). He is editor of *Broken Pencil* magazine, the guide to 'zines and alternative culture in Canada. He lives in Toronto. A modified version of "Stupid Jobs Are Good to Relax With" appeared originally in *This Magazine.*

KAREN OPAS · Forgetting Buckaroo Banzai's famous precept that, "No matter where you go, there you are" the author, born in Ireland, has lived in various parts. These include – but are not limited to – Jamaica, England, Ottawa, Sioux Lookout, Yellowknife, Cold Lake, the Yukon, Banff, Regina, and Vancouver. She regrets not sobering up before she decided that going $40,000 into debt for her MFA was a fine idea.

PAT PEDERSEN, poet/troublemaker, law-school drop-out, really scary employee, is currently working on an autobiographical horror piece, *The Last Resumé,* to be performed at an unemployment office near you.

LAURA PREFTES is a fiction writer, poet, and grant writer. With a string of bad jobs beneath her belt, she has plenty of material for future stories. "Death Would Be a Welcomed Visitor" is her first published story.

Sima Rabinowitz has had more than her share of jobs, bad and good. Her poetry and prose have appeared in a number of journals and anthologies. She has received a creative nonfiction award from the Loft in Minneapolis, and a fellowship in poetry from the Minnesota State Arts Board.

S. Reddick is a poet and bookseller who lives in Seattle, Washington. "Beet Line" is her first published story.

Jordan Robinson · Fully accredited, Jordan Robinson is serving an indefinite sentence at his longtime vespertine vocation. During daylight hours he is nearing completion of *Black The Impala*, a novel dealing with one death, one abduction, and twenty-something suicides, as seen through the eyes of a jobless young man who "seriously lacks initiative."

Rachel Rose has several special work skills, including phlebotomy, bread baking, diaper changing, cursing in Japanese, and cutting up little squares of fabric on big machines. She now lives in Montreal, writing and living from one $50 cheque to another, and following the philosophy that no job is better than a bad job.

Caroline C. Spear has published short stories in literary journals and has won several poetry contests. She spent fifteen years in corporate America before going back to school for a Masters in Teaching. Currently, she is Director of English at the Walt Whitman Academy in Ecuador and writes whenever she can.

Sandra E. Stevens currently works for a non-profit organization and teaches writing workshops in her spare time.

Peter Thompson · "I used to be a security guard, but I ain't no more."

Harry Vandervlist was born in Hamilton, Ontario. He teaches at the University of Calgary while writing what, and when, he can.

Marnie Woodrow is the author of two short fiction collections, *Why We Close Our Eyes When We Kiss* (1991) and *In The Spice House* (1996), from which "32 Flavours" appears. She is currently at work on a novel. You can contact her through her web-site at www.pneumatic.com/spicehouse. "32 Flavours" is reprinted with permission from McClelland & Stewart.

Zines About Jobs

Danzine
C/o Teresa Dulce
625 SW 10TH Ave., #464-C
Portland, OR · 97205

·

Fist City
C/o 2255 St. Mathieu #1206
Montreal, PQ · H3H 2J6

·

Guinea Pig Zero
PO Box 42531, Philadelphia, PA
19101

·

McJob
C/o Julie Peasley
PO Box 11794, Berkeley, CA
94772-2794

·

Temp Slave
C/o Keffo
PO Box 8284, Madison, WI
53708-8284

CARELLIN BROOKS
*is a freelance writer living in
Vancouver. Her bad jobs have included
construction worker, telephone solicitor, butcher
shop clerk, chat-line operator, coffee bar
girl, and supermarket slave,
among others.*